DON'T APOLOGIZE; DON'T SAY, "I'M SORRY."

DON'T APOLOGIZE; DON'T SAY, "I'M SORRY."

A BOOK ON PRACTICAL FORGIVENESS

RICK THOMAS

DON'T APOLOGIZE; DON'T SAY, "I'M SORRY."
A Book on Practical Forgiveness

ISBN 978-1-7323854-5-0

Rick Thomas

© 2025 Life Over Coffee

Unless otherwise noted, all Scripture references herein are from the English Standard Version, copyright © 2001 by Crossway, Inc. Used by permission. All rights reserved.

No part of this publication may be reproduced, stored in a retrieval system, or transmitted in any form or by any means without the express written permission of Life Over Coffee.

Edited by Sarah Hayhurst

Life Over Coffee
8595 Pelham Rd Ste 400 #406,
Greenville, SC 29615
LifeOverCoffee.com

If we say we have no sin, we deceive ourselves,
and the truth is not in us. If we confess our sins,
he is faithful and just to forgive us our sins and to
cleanse us from all unrighteousness. If we say we
have not sinned, we make him a liar,
and his word is not in us.
(1 John 1:8–10)

For additional resources, visit lifeovercoffee.com

Table of Contents

	Introduction	8
1	No Forgiveness	16
2	Don't Apologize	24
3	Sooty Offenders	32
4	Power of Unforgiveness	40
5	Pre-forgiveness	48
6	How Many Times	56
7	Un-asking Spouse	64
8	Manipulating Forgiveness	74
9	Lingering Unforgiveness	82
10	Past Sins	90
11	Forgiving Yourself	98
	Conclusion	106
	About the Author	111

Introduction

Forgiveness is the exclusive domain and the divinely given privilege of the redeemed. Non-Christians cannot be free from sin because God resists the proud, and He will not forgive any transgression until they humble themselves by becoming children of the light. Believers, however, can experience release from all their transgressions through forgiveness. This divinely granted gift is the means of grace that allows God's children to have relationships as He intended—with Him and others, bringing us to the all-important question: how do you live out forgiveness, practically speaking?

Cultural Forgiveness

Our point of departure with any forgiveness discussion should begin by delineating cultural and biblical forgiveness. Cultural forgiveness, usually framed as "I'm sorry," is like an empty add-on at the end of a conversation with a peripheral friend: "Hey, let's get together again!" We call it a southern expression: something we say but do not mean. It's a cultural courtesy conversational appendage that probably should be tossed into the miscellaneous file and labeled "little white lies." It lacks force, authenticity, clarity, and authority. Biblical forgiveness is a different animal. It is full of divine power, authentic realism, and clarity that will not find satisfaction until the guilty person experiences release from their transgressions.

Biblical forgiveness comes from the judge of the universe. It does not begin on the horizontal level between two human beings, looking to mitigate conflict. Sin-releasing forgiveness starts on the vertical plane—that divine space where the Sovereign God waits for the contrite of heart to enter His sacred sanctuary, seeking release for missing the mark. The first step in biblical forgiveness is always between the offender who has sinned and the offended, and the Lord is the first and preeminent offended person. If you want to end well with forgiveness, you must begin well. If you're going to experience release from any sin and all of the accompanying guilt and conviction that comes with a crime, you must make your requests known to God before you do anything else (2 Samuel 12:13).

Conditional Forgiveness

> If we confess our sins, he is faithful and just to forgive us our sins and to cleanse us from all unrighteousness.
>
> (1 John 1:9)

With the primary offended person in view, the passage in 1 John is a great place to think about the act and process of forgiveness. The operative word in that verse is conditional—If we confess our sins to the Lord, we may receive forgiveness for our sins. The implication of the opposite would also be true: if we do not acknowledge our sins to the Lord, He will be faithful and just not to forgive us of our sins and not to cleanse us from any unrighteousness. The condition for forgiveness hinges on whether the guilty person asks for forgiveness. A request for release must happen to experience release. We are not allowed to be sloppy in our forgiveness as though we can dismiss our sins by some other means.

To be forgiven outside of the parameters and power of the gospel would be a mockery of the gospel: Christ died for our sins (Romans 4:25). We must have the Lord's judicial approval for the obliteration of our sins. Therefore, we can conclude that we must ask for forgiveness to experience forgiveness, and we must first ask the Lord to be free and clear of our offenses. We also see this condition of forgiveness statement made in Romans regarding our salvation. Just as we can't experience forgiveness for sanctification sins without asking, we cannot receive salvation without asking.

> If you confess with your mouth that Jesus is Lord and believe in your heart that God raised him from the dead, you will be saved.
>
> (Romans 10:9)

Confessed Forgiveness

To confess means to agree with God about what we have done. We enter into the Lord's presence through prayer and agree with Him about what we did wrong. A confession is a way to get on the same page with the Lord. After we agree, we may ask Him to release us from the penalty that we justly deserve (Romans 6:23). If we do not request an offended person to free us from our offenses, we leave the potential forgiver in a threefold quandary:

- "I am not certain you are aware that you need forgiveness."
- "I am not certain you care about forgiveness."
- "I am not certain you want forgiveness."

Fixing our mistakes is not a passive activity. It takes engagement from both the offender and the offended. The Lord does not remove our mistakes without this kind of biblical reciprocality. If we humbly ask for forgiveness, we can be joyfully released from what we did wrong, which affirms the purpose of the cross. Jesus Christ willingly paid for our sins, which was ample enough to remove any penalties we may have accrued. There is so much money in the bank, and we can have full access to as much of it as we want as long as we humble ourselves, acknowledge our need, and request the gift.

But be warned. The offended person is not allowed to throw money at anyone that he wants to arbitrarily. Similarly, we cannot stand at the foot of the cross and arbitrarily release a person from their crimes when they have not owned what they did or requested release from the offense.

1. Forgiveness begins with God.
2. Forgiveness depends on agreement with God about what happened.
3. When the offender asks for forgiveness, he receives it.

Categorized Forgiveness

Understanding this "God first" priority of forgiveness is imperative because if God does not release us from our sins, we cannot receive the horizontal forgiveness we may seek from others. It would be the height of arrogance to think any of us could receive forgiveness from a person when the Almighty Lord has not first forgiven us. My forgiveness-granting is biblically meaningless if the sinner has not been forensically, legally, and divinely released by the ultimate offended power. It would be like me telling a person that he is a Christian when God has not regenerated him.

> "Hey, you don't have to ask the Lord to forgive you of your sins. I'll do that for you. Do you want to be saved? Great! You are saved! Go in peace."

Imagine being at your local courthouse and a convicted felon hobbled by you in an orange jumpsuit and chains. Before the criminal enters the courtroom, you go to the person and release him from his crimes. He is joyful and appreciative that you paid his debt to society. He continues into the courtroom only to discover that the judge is not as accommodating as you were. He sentences the felon to life in prison. Because God has not forgiven the person, any pronouncement we make about him is irrelevant—unless all we are looking for is some form of partial cultural agreement to put the relational tension behind us.

If we sin against someone and ask them to forgive us, but do not ask God to forgive us, then we are not forgiven in the way we need forgiveness because we are still guilty before God. You could think of it like categories: the Lord is always the primary category, and everyone else is secondary. God is always the utmost offended person when sin happens, and until the offender reconciles that relationship, all terrestrial confessions will be inadequate. No one can grant forgiveness to us, as though we can be free from the sin committed, if we have not asked God to release us from it.

Complete Forgiveness

This link in the sequence brings us to the sphere of confession. With the good Lord's full pardon of our crimes, we are now ready to approach all the other people within our spheres of offense. Think about it like the same size circles that stack on top of each other. The first circle is the sphere of offense. We have to determine all the people that we have offended. Because God is always the offended party, He is always within our circle of offense. All sin offends God. No exceptions. But there may be other people within the sphere of offense.

Consider it like a group of people in white clothing standing on a sidewalk. As you pass by them in your vehicle, you hit a mud puddle and splash some of them with dirty road water. You go back to find out who all you dirtied by your actions. That is your sphere of offense. The people you offended—sphere of offense—should be the same number you want to confess your sin to—sphere of confession. God is always offended by your sin, and other people may be in the offense sphere. There will be other people not within your sphere of offense. There is no pressing need to let them know what you have done—at least, you should not seek their forgiveness.

Then there are times when you cannot ask a person to forgive you for what you did to them (Romans 12:18). Suppose you had a dysfunctional relationship with your father who passed away. His death makes relationship reconciliation impossible. In such cases where transactional forgiveness is impossible, God provides grace. Ask the Lord to forgive you for the wrongs in that relationship while sharing your attitude of forgiveness with Him—a heart that wants to forgive and be free from what happened but cannot transact the forgiveness. In time you should be able to rest in His grace. You have done all that you can do (Romans 12:18).

Convicted Forgiveness

When you are asking someone to forgive you, it is incumbent that you try to remove any doubt or speculation about the genuineness of your confession and your request for forgiveness. You do not want to make it harder for the offended person to forgive you. They are already struggling with what you did. Don't add to that struggle by being casual or flippant about forgiveness. If your sin has broken you, you should be willing to do anything to make it right. (See Psalm 51:1-19 and Luke 15:17-24) One of the ways you can do this is by bringing a clear and unassailable case against yourself regarding what you did. Here is a sample of what that could look like:

> I know I have offended you. I have sinned against God and you. The Spirit of God has convicted me for what I did, and I cannot rest until I'm completely free from my transgressions. I'm so sorry that my sin has hurt you. I wish to take it back, but realize I can't undo it. I hope you can forgive me for my actions. I sinned when I [specific sin]. It did not honor the Lord's name or bless you in any way. I throw myself at your mercy and will not be able to move forward until you grant me forgiveness. Will you forgive me?

While it's not necessary to parrot this sample confession, it is essential to have the attitude that this confession and request for forgiveness communicate. Your confession must be pneumatic as you and the Spirit of God collaborate on how you want to present your case against yourself to another person. You don't want to be nonchalant, haphazard, flippant, vague, or rote. Make it as straightforward as possible for the offended person to forgive you. You can do this if your sin has genuinely broken you, which you will convey by asking them to release you from it.

Call to Action

1. **CONDITIONAL FORGIVENESS:** You may receive forgiveness *if* you ask. Are you hesitant to confess your sins to those you have offended? If so, why are you this way?
2. **CONFESSED FORGIVENESS:** Do you make it clear to God and others what you did, so they can quickly agree with you about what you did? If not, why not?
3. **CATEGORIZED FORGIVENESS:** Are there times when you never ask the Lord to forgive you, though you do ask others? If so, how will you change?
4. **COMPLETE FORGIVENESS:** Do you seek out all those you offended so you can reconcile with them for the sin you committed?
5. **CONVICTED FORGIVENESS:** What is your general deportment when making a case against yourself to another person? Is there anything you need to change about conveying the seriousness of your transgressions? If so, what is your plan for change?

1

No Forgiveness

Forgiveness is one of the most challenging concepts for Christians to come to terms with, especially when someone has hurt them. The recipients of unjust and unkind actions experience legitimate disappointment that does not always go away quickly. Fortunately, we do not have to despair: we have a suffering Savior who went through many unjust trials, leaving us a template for thinking about and responding to when someone sins against us. Of course, as you might imagine, the pathway to follow Him through suffering has complexities and challenges, but there is grace for this as we can read and learn from Peter's perspective on the Savior's suffering.

Follow the Leader

For this is a gracious thing, when, mindful of God, one endures sorrows while suffering unjustly. For what credit is it if, when you sin and are beaten for it, you endure? But if when you do good and suffer for it, you endure, this is a gracious thing in the sight of God. For to this, you have been called, because Christ also suffered for you, leaving you an example, so that you might follow in his steps. He committed no sin, neither was deceit found in his mouth. When he was reviled, he did not revile in return; when he suffered, he did not threaten, but

continued entrusting himself to him who judges justly.
(1 Peter 2:19–23)

Peter wants us to learn as we walk in the steps of Jesus. Though your hurt might seem too painful at this moment, you can emulate Christ as a beloved child of the Father (Ephesians 5:1). Because of our great salvation, anyone can be free from the relational problems that entangle them—including unjust suffering. But beware: freedom comes with a price (Galatians 5:1). The smell of death is always in the air when forgiveness is the need of the hour, which is why there is such an active call in God's Word to die to ourselves.

If anyone would come after me, let him deny himself and take up his cross daily and follow me.
(Luke 9:23)

Ready to Die?

Forgiveness is a complex message, but it is the perfect response for relational reconciliation. It starts with a heart of forgiveness, which is forgiving offenders attitudinally. Of course, the goal is transactional forgiveness if they are willing to cooperate. Our lives and internal soul noise will never be exemplary without learning and applying attitudinal and transactional forgiveness. Some of the saddest people you will ever meet are those who refuse to forgive those who have sinned against them. I have counseled scores of these hurt people; their stories are heartbreaking. People have profoundly hurt them, and their pain is real and unending. Any discussion about forgiveness with them is nearly always met with deep emotional angst and, sometimes, hostility. Many of these fellow strugglers do not need a rebuke but a gentle, courageous, and biblical caregiver to help restore them (Galatians 6:1).

With as much patience and compassion as you can muster, you want to lead them to the only freedom they can have, which they will find through Christ's attitude of forgiveness of those who sinned against Him. To care for an offended soul, you must steward their two realities: the hurt they are experiencing and their need to forgive the person who hurt them. Sometimes uncaring caregivers will press a person to forgive someone when they cannot do it—at that time. They may mouth the words, "I forgive you," but it won't be authentic because a forgiving heart did not produce the words (Luke 6:45). Though they must not hold on to unforgiveness forever, it takes time to work through the complexity of the soul to let an offense go, even if they are only releasing the offender from the heart (attitudinally) because the offender has never come forward to transact relational forgiveness (transactional).

Foolishness of God

> *For the foolishness of God is wiser than men, and the weakness of God is stronger than men.*
> *(1 Corinthians 1:25)*

Like nearly everything else in the Christian life, forgiveness is upside down. Paul talked about how God's ways appear weak or foolish compared to ours (Isaiah 55:8–9). The cross of Christ was amazingly foolish to His disciples. It was so hard for them to comprehend that they ran away when they were supposed to stay put and make a stand for their leader. A dying man on a tree was counter-intuitive to their beliefs and hopes. "Wait! What? He is supposed to rule the world. He can't die now." In time, the disciples began to see how the gospel was not what they thought it was. After a season of re-envisioning, they reacquainted themselves with the "foolishness and weakness of God." And when they did, it began to look like real power and true wisdom from another kingdom. Forgiveness is one of those counter-intuitive planks in the gospel's platform. God calls us to forgive each other attitudinally or transactionally, regardless of the pain, regret, or disappointment.

One of the ironies of unforgiveness is how the offended is the one experiencing unending suffering when they don't forgive. Unwillingness to forgive the perpetrator of the sin will only perpetuate the offended's suffering. It's like the incremental sipping of bitter water. Each time the victim thinks about what someone did to them while holding on to an unforgiving attitude, they hurt themselves more. In most situations, the unforgiving person does not fully realize how holding on to unforgiveness makes things worse for them. Unforgiveness never makes things better because God will not bless anyone who persists in holding on to an unforgiving attitude toward anyone (James 4:6; Romans 1:18). Paul teaches us how the Lord's displeasure rains down from heaven on any person who presses His truth out of their lives. That was the testimony of King David. The longer he kept silent about the sin he carried in his heart, the more he experienced the Lord's wrathful displeasure.

> For when I kept silent, my bones wasted away through my groaning all day long. For day and night, your hand was heavy upon me; my strength was dried up as by the heat of summer.
> (Psalm 32:3–4)

Practical Deterioration

If the unforgiving person continues to hold on to unforgiveness, he will accrue the deterioration of both the body and the soul. Ironically, the perpetrator (the offender) of the suffering is usually unaware of this soul deterioration effect on the one he has hurt. Unforgiveness is just one sin, but it will never hibernate in autonomy. It's like cancer when left to its own devices. A gathering constellation of sins will emerge with the intent of devouring its prey (1 Peter 5:8). Here is a non-exhaustive list of some of the more common problems that unforgiving people experience. You can use this list for self-analysis as you examine yourself to see if you are holding on to unforgiveness toward another person.

- **Gossip:** The unforgiving person regularly talks negatively about others, especially those who hurt them.
- **Criticalness:** The unforgiving person tends to express more negativity than positivity about life.
- **Joylessness:** You would not characterize the unforgiving person as happy, joyful, or hopeful.
- **Self-deceived:** The unforgiving person is unwilling to see their situation with biblical clarity.
- **Lying:** The unforgiving person tends to spin the truth to put themselves in a better light.
- **Anger:** The unforgiving person exhibits various forms of unrighteous anger.
- **Bitterness:** The unforgiving person's ongoing anger eventually turns into sourness. (This is the downward spiral effect of unrepentant sin.)
- **Offended:** The unforgiving person is defensive and quick to retaliate because they view life through the lens of their hurt.

Sin will not discriminate. Just because someone is offended does not mean they are impervious to sin's multi-faceted encroachments. I gave only a few possibilities of what can happen to the recipient of someone else's offenses. Refusing to forgive a fellow sinner is a posture that perpetuates pain while keeping the offended person in a self-erected prison.

Choose Freedom

Living with the freedom of a forgiving spirit is one of the hardest things you'll ever do, especially if someone has hurt you. I vividly remember working through the process of forgiving my sister-in-law for murdering my brother. That process did not come easy. I struggled to take my soul to task, especially since she was not asking for forgiveness. Without the opportunity to forgive her transactionally, I had to wrestle with God to free my soul from the hurt I carried in my attitude toward her. In time, I was able to forgive her attitudinally. I do not know if she has asked God to forgive her (1 John 1:9). I hope she has. She has not received mine because she has never asked for it, but her lack of asking did not stop me from being fully released from what she did to our family. God has done miraculous work in my heart, for which I am eternally grateful.

Though I can still cry when I think about my brother, I have been set free from the soul entanglements that easily capture the unforgiving heart. Perhaps you are struggling to forgive someone who has hurt you. It's a pain I do not need to explain because you are living it each day. The reminders are everywhere, and your mind can be quickly captivated by what that person did to you (2 Corinthians 10:3–6). To walk out of that dark tunnel, you must pray often. And as you pray, you will need to ask yourself a few hard questions, all of which center on why you are unwilling to forgive the person who has hurt you. When I did my self-examination, there were at least seven reasons why I was reluctant to let it go. I will share those reasons with you while asking you about each one. Will you reflect on these questions as you take them to the Lord—especially if you struggle with unforgiveness toward someone?

- **Punishment:** Do you have any desire for someone to punish the offender?
- **Fearfulness:** Are you afraid that forgiving them will permit them to hurt you again?
- **Unbelief:** Do you believe God will fully take care of what happened to you?
- **Control:** Does unforgiveness allow you to stay in control of the situation?
- **Righteousness:** Do you believe you are better than the offender? (See Isaiah 64:6; Romans 3:10–12.)
- **Acceptance:** Do you manipulate the sympathy others can give you for what happened to you?
- **Identity:** Are you finding your identity in your suffering rather than in Christ?

Call to Action

Only the Lord can grant the repentance necessary for you to let go of unforgiveness. He does this by working His good will in you while expecting you to work it out practically (Philippians 2:12-13). The call to repentance is both a passive and active action. (See 2 Corinthians 3:18; James 1:22.) God grants forgiveness (2 Timothy 2:24-25), and we are to respond to His good work. We all have hurt others, and others have sinned against us. I trust that you will model your Savior as you appropriate His grace in areas where you need to change. Here are a few questions to consider as you process this information. If you have a friend who will walk with you, please get with that person and pray through this book's content, but let's start with these questions.

1. Have you been sinned against by someone? Has a person hurt you? Describe what happened.
2. What do you think about that person? What is your attitude toward them?
3. Will you forgive them attitudinally, even though they have not come to you seeking your forgiveness for what they did to you? If not, what is keeping you from doing this?
4. If you cannot at least forgive them from the heart, will you seek the help you need until you can accomplish this? Will you fight for your freedom in Christ?

Take your time. Forgiveness is not something you can accelerate; it will take time, so there is no need to hurry. After you have worked through my questions and discussed them with a friend, please continue through the remainder of this book.

2

Don't Apologize

In our culture today, the phrase "I'm sorry" has become our first response when we sin against each other. The term has nearly wholly replaced biblical forgiveness. It is a passive statement that does not require the offender and offended to engage in meaningful, biblical transactional forgiveness. Perhaps "I'm sorry" is a good start in relational reconciliation, but the phrase will never complete the needed task when sin is in play and grace is available. Transactional forgiveness is the antidote that neutralizes and obliterates any sin, setting the stage for those in the transgressive dust-up to reconcile with each other.

A Sorry Illustration

"I'm sorry" terminology has taken over almost all relational indiscretions, which becomes particularly problematic when the depth and extent of our offenses toward each other need more biblical power to redress legitimate crimes against the Divine and others (Romans 1:16). Many of the Christians that I have counseled do not practice biblical forgiveness in their relationships, partly because they don't know any better and partly because "I'm sorry" is the path of least resistance. When I ask them to walk me through how they forgive each other, in nearly all cases, they present some version of the "I'm sorry" mantra. "I'm sorry" does not have the divine efficacy to neutralize and remove actual sin.

"I'm sorry" is better suited for non-sin events like running out the door and closing it in front of my wife while not realizing she was behind me. My heart's motivation was not sinful, as though I was thinking about how to punish her. It was a brain cramp at best that did not serve her but never rose to the level of transgressing God's Word. In such a case, it would be more appropriate to say, "I'm sorry," to express my love for her and my desire not to harm her. To be sorrowful is good, but to equate a biblical transgression with a mistake is too much pesticide for non-threatening weeds. Inappropriate discretions do not need repentance because you have not sinned. Thus, I can make a case for saying, "I'm sorry," but never when there is sin and the two people need to enter a transactional moment.

A Forgiveness Illustration

> What causes quarrels, and what causes fights among you? Is it not this, that your passions are at war within you? You desire and do not have, so you murder. You covet and cannot obtain, so you fight and quarrel. You do not have, because you do not ask.
>
> (James 4:1–2)

Let's spice up the scene a bit. Suppose I was angry with my wife, and we both were heading out the door. I passed across the threshold first and slammed the door in front of her as she was attempting to exit. Saying "I'm sorry" would be a woefully incomplete and unbiblical response. I desired to hurt her through sinful anger. James identified my problem as a wicked heart at war within, manifesting as sinful anger toward my wife. James would say I have transgressed God's Word, offended the Lord, and sinned against my wife. He would appeal to me to do the more profound heart work to root out such offenses, which would begin with cleaning up the mess by asking God and my wife to forgive me. Only biblical forgiveness can communicate what is required when a sin like this is involved.

- Forgiveness heightens the awareness that I sinned.
- Forgiveness is part of the process of repentance.
- Forgiveness allows the sinner to be free from what he did.
- Forgiveness allows the offended to release the sinner from his crime.
- Forgiveness affirms the testimony of the gospel: Christ died for our sins.
- Forgiveness brings glory to God by not minimizing the need for Him to send His Son.
- Forgiveness fosters humility.
- Forgiveness removes sin between two people.
- Forgiveness gives a death blow to sin's advances.
- Forgiveness pictures to others how to deal with sin.

"I'm sorry" does not allow two people in a relational dust-up to accomplish any of these things. "I'm sorry" sucks the life and the force out of repentance while leaving the offense unresolved. "I'm sorry" is not a request for the offended to do anything. "I'm sorry" is a statement that does not require a response from the hurt person. Forgiveness is different. It requires the offender and the offended to actively engage each other for the express purpose of neutralizing and removing the sin that occurred between them. Technically speaking, "I'm sorry" does not require a response because it implies the act committed was in the realm of "no harm, no foul." Asking for forgiveness puts a responsibility on the person offended to respond to the request of the offender asking for forgiveness.

Start with Confession

If you go back to my slamming the door in front of my wife illustration where the sin of anger was in play, you can now see how "I'm sorry" won't cut it. To say "I'm sorry" is unbiblical, un-releasing, and unkind because there was an objective sin between the offended and the offender. If I do not ask Lucia for forgiveness, she would not have had the opportunity to release me from my sin. The same applies to the Lord: if I do not ask God to forgive me, He cannot free me from what I did. (See 1 John 1:9.) Furthermore, I would leave Lucia with my sin affecting her soul, with no opportunity for her to deal with it transactionally. Minimally, she could forgive me attitudinally by working it out with the Lord (Luke 23:34). Still, without transactional forgiveness that removes sin, our relationship would have tension, which would keep us from enjoying true koinonia (communication).

The Plot Thickens: In addition to Lucia not being free from the effects of my sin, I would never be released from it either. Like a cancerous cyst on my body, I would always be vulnerable to sin's deadly possibilities because the power of the gospel never neutralized it. The only recourse would be to humble myself before Lucia and the Lord, pleading for their forgiveness. There has never been a time in our marriage when it was acceptable to apologize to Lucia by saying, "I'm sorry" for my sin toward her and leaving it at that. Though "I'm sorry" may be an excellent start to a forgiveness conversation, it should never be the warp and woof of that conversation. I must ask for forgiveness from God and Lucia, and they must grant it.

> If we confess our sins, he is faithful and just to forgive us our sins and to cleanse us from all unrighteousness.
>
> (1 John 1:9)

The forgiveness conversation always begins with a confession. To confess our sin to another person means that we agree with that person that what we did was wrong. The word "confess" means "to agree." We cannot experience biblical forgiveness without confessing—without agreeing with those we have offended that what we did was wrong (sinful). The person sinned against—the offended—needs to know that we understand how bad what we did was to them. We want to make it crystal clear in their minds that what we did was awful, wrong, and unjustified. All people within the offense's sphere need to agree regarding what happened.

Prosecute Me

It is as though the offender is a prosecuting attorney, prosecuting himself for the crime he committed. This need is where half-hearted apologies will never work. Have you ever been asked to forgive someone, but you were left wondering if they perceived how what they did was wrong or how bad what they did hurt you? Biblical forgiveness does not leave anything to chance. It is as though the convicted person is on a mission to find release from his crime, and he will not rest until he is fully exonerated (forgiven) by God and any other person that he has offended. This biblical worldview is why he wants to be actionable, accurate, and articulate in how he goes about prosecuting himself. This kind of confession puts everyone involved on the same page—they all agree.

Proper confession positions all appropriate parties to ask for forgiveness, grant, and receive it, so it's crucial to own the specifics of our sin by naming and claiming it. Do not let any person you have sinned against go away wondering whether or not you were fully aware of what you did, that you understood how what you did hurt them, and that your request for forgiveness does not lack clarity because of a murky confession. In short, you're bringing a solid case against yourself, making it impossible for them not to forgive you. Here is a suggestive template that frames this concept.

> Lucia, what I did to you was wrong. I was angry when I responded to you that way. It did not please God and did not edify you (Ephesians 4:29). My speech was corrupting and hurt you. I wanted what I wanted more than what God wanted or what you deserved from me. I love you, and I do understand what I did. Will you forgive me?

Honor the Gospel

What I am describing here is a far cry from apologizing or saying, "I'm sorry." What I am illustrating takes you to the heart of the gospel. The gospel informs us that sin is actual and binds souls, whether the soul belongs to the offended or the offender. The gospel tells us that there is empowering favor for our sins. But we are responsible for biblically cleaning up our messes before God and others. If we do not admit our sins, seek forgiveness, or require others to forgive us, we have dishonored the gospel by muting its power and marginalizing its purpose.

The point of the gospel is to release sinners from their sins. Christ came to free the captive, which happens at salvation and for the rest of our lives in our progressive sanctification. If we embrace our culture's habit of saying, "I'm sorry," we may as well embrace their Jesus too: He was merely a good man, but not the Son of God who died for and obliterated our sins. Christians know better, and we can do better. Don't apologize. Don't say, "I'm sorry," when more is needed. Ask for forgiveness when you sin, and freely forgive those who ask for it: that is the power of the gospel working in us.

Call to Action

1. Why is transactional forgiveness better than saying, "I'm sorry?"
2. Illustrate a situation with a friend where it's proper to say "I'm sorry" without asking for forgiveness.
3. Is it hard for you to confess your sin and ask for forgiveness? If so, why so? What keeps you from humbly asking the person you offend to forgive you?
4. Think through your past relational dust-ups. Are you more apt to default to an apology or an "I'm sorry" when confession and forgiveness would be better? If you answered yes, what does it say about your understanding the gospel—Christ dying for sin?
5. How prosecutorial of yourself are you when seeking forgiveness from someone? How easy do you make it for them to forgive you because you make it clear to them? Why is it necessary to help them forgive you?
6. Have you ever forgiven someone even though you questioned their sincerity? How will you work to clear up future ambiguity?
7. Would you characterize your closest relationships as repentant relationships? If not, what is your plan to strengthen those relationships?
8. Do you live in a confessional family environment? Are the people in your home habitually asking for forgiveness when they sin? If not, why not?

Don't Apologize

3

Sooty Offenders

Biff destroyed his marriage. Shortly after that, he experienced conviction from God for what he did. His repentance was genuine, as affirmed by his pastor, several other church leaders, and two of his workmates. In response to the Lord's maneuvering in his heart and with the blessing and oversight of his pastor, Biff made an authentic confession to God and his wife, Mable. In a strange turn of events, the man who destroyed his family wants to be part of God's restoration team to put it back together again. Analogous to Christ and us, the offenders cooperate with the offended for God's glory, our benefit, and the good of others.

Sooty-handed Offender

Along with his confession and forgiveness request, he then asked the most profound question of all—to help restore what he had destroyed. Genuine repentance is more than confessing your sin and asking for forgiveness. While those two elements of repentance are essential, there is more to do to change completely (Ephesians 4:28-29). True repentance is turning 180 degrees from where you were while embarking in the opposite direction (Luke 15:17-20). Sin had entangled and estranged Biff (Galatians 6:1). He actively participated in a hedonistic lifestyle. Now he is walking out repentance, which means he is actively walking away from his ungodly life.

Part of this process was his request to join his wife in a mutual effort to rebuild what he had destroyed. Let me illustrate: suppose someone burnt your house to the ground. Let's further suppose the person genuinely repented as Biff is doing. He comes to you and asks for your forgiveness. He wants to help you rebuild the destroyed home as part of his repentance. There you are, standing in the charred rubble of his sin. Your tears have cut paths across your soot-covered face. Biff is in the yard looking at you. You see the soot on his hands and the gasoline container at his feet. With smoke in the air and destruction all around you, there is a sincere request for forgiveness. What are you going to do with your sooty-handed offender?

Several years ago, I used this burnt house illustration with a couple during counseling. The husband was guilty of sinning against God and his wife. He repented, which began with a positive change process that several others close to him affirmed, including one of his pastors. His wife was angry over what happened. After a while, she became bitter. Prolonged anger turns to bitterness if you do not submit it to the power of the gospel, which is what happened to that wife. No amount of conversation would change her mind. She stayed angry for several years until she finally filed for divorce. The husband continued to walk out repentance, even though she was unwilling to forgive him.

The Practical Gospel

I realized what I was asking her to do. It is one of the hardest things anyone can do. When you are hurt deeply by someone, even if the perpetrator of the sin is genuine in his repentance, it takes other-worldly favor to forgive the offender. That wife would not consider it, and I was not placing an artificial timeline on her to change her mind. With much patience and prayer, we appealed and waited. She would not change. She chose divorce. This problem brings you to the heart of the gospel. One of the most important diagnostic questions we could ever ask ourselves is our willingness to forgive someone who has sinned against us authentically. I'm talking about a person who is living in genuine repentance. I realize this situation can raise a lot of other questions about forgiveness. Here are three of the more common ones:

- What if the offender does not ask for forgiveness?
- What if their repentance is not genuine?
- How long must I work through my hurt before forgiving someone authentically?

These are crucial questions that go beyond the scope of this chapter. I have written extensively on forgiveness, especially those questions which you may find on our website. This chapter deals with only one aspect of forgiveness—our need to forgive those genuinely seeking it. To withhold forgiveness when it is genuinely requested will put us in an adversarial relationship with God (James 4:6) while never reconciling our relationship with the offender. Perhaps considering these three verses will help to keep our minds calibrated rightly on the gospel's practicality.

> For if you forgive others their trespasses, your heavenly Father will also forgive you, but if you do not forgive others their trespasses, neither will your Father forgive your trespasses.
> (Matthew 6:14–15)

> And whenever you stand praying, forgive, if you have anything against anyone, so that your Father also who is in heaven may forgive you your trespasses.
> (Mark 11:25)

Gospel Offenders

In the case of an ongoing relationship like marriage, true forgiveness does not stop with the transaction. In marriage, we forgive the offender for their sins against us and allow them to partner with us in the restorative process. Our goal is to rebuild what the sinner destroyed. I am describing one of the most profound facets of the gospel. In my illustration about the burned home, the Father, Son, and Spirit represent the offended party—the victim of the crime. We are the sooty-handed offenders who opposed God, even to the point of putting Jesus on the cross (Acts 2:36). Sin had captured us (Romans 5:12, 2:10-12, 23). We led Jesus to the slaughter, like a sheep before its shearers (Isaiah 53:7).

Our actions caused Him to be despised, afflicted, pierced, and punished (Isaiah 53:3-5). We burned down His house. It was because of our heinous acts against God that He gave us the gospel (Isaiah 53:10). His great love provided us an opportunity to repent and experience release from our sins (Romans 5:8). We, the accused, were freed from the guilt and punishment that we so justly deserved. "For freedom, Christ has set us free" (Galatians 5:1). But the story does not stop there; it is even sweeter than being forgiven and set free from our crimes.

The Lord has given us the privilege of joining the one we offended for the great work of bringing other people to Christ's freedom. The offenders—you and me—cooperate with the offended—Father, Son, and Spirit—in this great gospel work. We are ambassadors for Christ (2 Corinthians 5:20) as God makes His appeal to many sooty-handed offenders through us. Once enemies of the cross, now we are His freedom fighters. This opportunity is amazing grace. This privilege is the power of the gospel (Romans 1:16).

> But Saul, still breathing threats and murder against the disciples of the Lord, went to the high priest.
>
> (Acts 9:1)

Gospel Partners

When Paul was Saul, his pastime was harassing Christians. He hated them. Acts 9:1 talks about his hatred for Christians as breathing threats and murder toward the disciples of the Lord. Then Paul became a Christian. After being born a second time (John 3:7), he started working with the people he previously persecuted. As you can imagine, they were initially nervous about working with him (Acts 9:13). But they chose not to withhold forgiveness when he requested it. They reconciled with Paul and became partners in the gospel (Philippians 1:5). But it gets better.

Today, the persecutor of the Christians—Paul—and the formerly persecuted Christians worship the Savior together in heaven. The power of the gospel testifies that we can experience reconciliation today and throughout eternity. The question for us is whether or not we will seek to forgive others when we have the opportunity to do so. Forgiveness words are not empty words. They are redemptive words that find their origin in transformed hearts (Luke 6:45). I am talking about genuine forgiveness extended toward other people who want to experience release from their sin. These people were like you and me when we asked God to forgive us.

One of the ways that you can know if your forgiveness words are redemptive words is if your forgiveness and reconciliation move into a gospel partnership. This coupling of the offender and offended is essential for married partners. When Lucia and I sin against each other, we must do more than forgive each other. We must be reconciled and restored for gospel purposes. We can't go our separate ways. Sometimes, all you will do is experience forgiveness and reconciliation. You will not continue in a gospel partnership because you don't have a relationship with the other person. In such situations, it's unnecessary to keep relating or try to be best buddies, but in the case of marriage, we must fight for the one-flesh union.

Withholding Forgiveness

Those who forgave Paul for his actions went beyond forgiveness by partnering with him in the gospel mission. Whether or not you are to partner with someone, you must ensure that your forgiveness words are not in vain. It would be best to use redemptive words affirmed by transformative actions that move two people toward reconciliation and restoration. There are two ways to withhold forgiveness from someone, both of which will take our minds captive (2 Corinthians 10:3-6) while straining our relationships.

- We withhold transactional forgiveness when someone asks us to forgive them.
- We withhold attitudinal forgiveness when someone is not asking us for forgiveness.

In this chapter, I am speaking specifically about transactional forgiveness between two people where there has been an offender and the offended. In such situations, the offended must not withhold forgiveness when the offender asks. Transactional forgiveness begins with the offended's attitude. It must be a genuine, transformed heart of mercy toward the sinner. They are not releasing them from their offense until they ask, but they cannot succumb to the capturing effects of what sinners have done to them. Of course, if the offenders do not ask for forgiveness, the offended must beg God to give them favor to keep from drowning in the anger and bitterness of an unforgiving heart. There is too much at stake to hold on to unforgiveness toward those who have hurt us.

- Unforgiveness will capture our hearts and ruin our minds.
- Unforgiveness will strain and ruin our relationships.
- Unforgiveness will negatively impact those who observe our Christianity.
- Unforgiveness will smear the fame of God.
- Unforgiveness will put us in an adversarial relationship with God.

Call to Action

Has someone hurt you? I realize that is an unnecessary question; of course, they have. Someone has offended all of us, and we all have hurt others. Fallen people cannot live in a fallen world and not hurt others. It is a sad outcome of our fallen lives. All people hurt people. The better discussion is whether or not you will forgive transactionally or attitudinally. One way to know if you have forgiven someone is by how you think and talk about them.

1. How do you think and talk about the person who has hurt you? Are you bitter, critical, cynical, or any other form of anger toward them? Or do you sense biblical pity for them, knowing you're no different apart from the grace of God in your life?
2. Are you willing to forgive those who are asking you for forgiveness? This response is a transactional event between two people.
3. Are you willing to attitudinally forgive those who have yet to ask for your forgiveness and who may never ask you for forgiveness? Attitudinal forgiveness does not release them from their guilt but frees the offended from the control of their sin.

4. Is there someone in your life with whom you are withholding forgiveness? If so, how long will you continue to withhold your forgiveness? Consider this question in light of Christ's refusal to withhold His mercy from you.
5. Who has "burned down your house?" Are you ready to show mercy to them? Read this passage.

> Then his master summoned him and said to him, "You wicked servant! I forgave you all that debt because you pleaded with me. And should not you have had mercy on your fellow servant, as I had mercy on you?" And in anger, his master delivered him to the jailers, until he should pay all his debt. So also my heavenly Father will do to every one of you if you do not forgive your brother from your heart.
> (Matthew 18:32–35)

4

Power of Unforgiveness

Sometimes in some relationships, a person will utilize unforgiveness as a tool for self-protection. They weaponize unforgiveness, even if they do so unwittingly. They might hold on to unforgiveness because they have been hurt so many times by the same person, usually a spouse or a parent. They are frustrated and disappointed and believe there is no other recourse but a self-reliant means of self-protection. Suppose you sense this is happening with a friend. In that case, you must tread courageously and carefully as you help them see how they are complicating—even self-sabotaging—an already complicated matter.

Self-Prescribed Cancer

When forgiveness is the right option, but the hurt person chooses unforgiveness, it could be a false security measure to protect themselves from future suffering. It won't work, at least long-term. The person holding on to the anger and hurt cannot see (or is unwilling to see) how unforgiveness is self-prescribed cancer; it will eat away at their unforgiving soul. Their unforgiveness suggests two things: "I will not let you close to hurt me again, and I will not let you be free from what you did." It is proactively protective and punitive. No one should hold on to any sin, no matter how justified or insecure they feel. They must understand that unforgiveness is a form of anger that will take revenge on the soul. It will tangle their soul in knots (Galatians 6:1) as they punish those who have hurt them (Luke 23:34).

Have you been tempted to withhold forgiveness from someone? If you have, the best thing to do is seek help from those who can walk you through letting go of self-punishment and punitive anger. No matter what has happened to you, holding on to anger and unforgiveness will wear you down to a nub. It is as unwise as it is un-gospel, something our friends—Biff and Mable—learned the hard way. Their marriage was your typical looks-okay-on-the-outside relationship. But the inside was full of loneliness and low-grade hostility toward each other—until all Hades broke loose, the day the tables turned when Mable became empowered by unforgiveness.

Biff was a likable guy. Every time they went to counseling, he and the counselor hit it off, which would infuriate Mable. It was one of the reasons she stopped going. She later said, "Why go? He will go, put on his people-pleasing smile, and the counselor will wonder why I have a problem within twenty minutes. They like Biff because everybody likes Biff. They come to the same conclusion: he married a nagging discontent. So why bother?" The consensus was that his perceived spiritual maturity and humble servant's heart were something others should emulate. When he wasn't running his moderately successful business, he volunteered at his local church, leading not one but two men's Bible studies. The pastors loved him because he was free labor, and they saw Biff as a model Christian.

Spilled the Beans

It didn't help that they were too busy to look beyond the surface of his life. "Besides, the squeaky wheel gets the grease," and Biff never squeaked. Except for one glaring problem: Mable could not stand Biff. It was their hidden marital secret. She had lived with a low-grade hatred toward her husband for nearly twenty years. The only reasons she would not leave him were the stigma of divorce—"what it would do to their children"—the hassle of starting over, or "God hates divorce, you know," she said sarcastically. Mable's issue with Biff was pretty straightforward: he was a hypocrite. Biff was a self-absorbed people-pleaser who learned how to manage the gap between who he was and the person he presented himself to be. The problem for Biff and Mable was that he could not maintain his hypocrisy entirely, and as these things tend to go, the one place where he could not keep up a front was in his home.

That was okay with Biff. Mostly. He counted on Mable not to spill the beans, and Mable acquiesced because living in a lie was the path of least resistance. With no public chink in his spiritual armor, she silently suffered through it all. Though she had an occasional short fuse, in the depths of her heart, she knew something more sinister was in play. Give a hypocrite an inch, and he'll take a mile. The problem was that she could not pinpoint where it all led. Coupled with this low-grade anger toward him was her fear that whatever he was into would devastate her. That awareness gave her another reason not to look too deeply into Biff's life. For her, ignorance was an uncomfortable but acceptable bliss.

It was late on a Monday afternoon when Mable emptied the home office trashcan that she noticed a receipt from a strip club. It was unmistakable. Her heart beat furiously, and her mouth went dry. Her ignorance became knowledge, and the news crushed her soul. Her tension was between walking out the door for good and confronting Biff with the truth she found in the trash. She chose to engage, and not surprisingly, Biff was shocked, though he quickly regained his equilibrium and went into his people-pleasing routine. Mable was not impressed; she had seen that shtick too many times. She stood firm. After a few days of drawn-out arguments, denials, confrontations, and threats, Biff finally came clean.

The Wounded's Weapon

He told Mable what she later recalled as the worst news of her life. He was into porn. She was devastated. In time, Biff went to counseling and came completely clean about his sin. Remarkably he chose not to stick with his well-worn people-pleasing routine, and he received favor from the Lord (James 4:6), which gave him what he needed to walk out repentance. Biff always wanted to be free from his sin. He later said he was glad it came out because he did not have the integrity or the courage to let others know how he struggled. Mable, on the other hand, was struggling. Even a year later, she was unwilling to forgive Biff. Mable was angry, critical, bitter, self-justifying, and self-righteous. Twelve months later, she would not let it go in her heart or marriage. Mable had been hurting for two decades. Twenty years! She also had been stewing in anger for most of that time.

From her perspective, forgiveness seemed too easy for Biff. Even when others made heartfelt appeals for her to let it go, she would not relent. She knew she was right—or wanted others to believe she was. She felt people did not understand. How could they? They did not live with Biff, and only a few knew the soul-rending effect porn could have on a spouse. She saw Biff for who he was—a hypocritical fool, which soured her belief in his genuine repentance. As she said, "He did not willingly confess his sins; I caught him!"

She believed he probably never would have confessed his sin if she had not found the strip club receipt. She was more than likely correct. Biff even said as much. Though he wanted help, he was too weak in his faith to trust God enough with the most powerful and darkest secret of his life. Plus, he enjoyed his shiny Christian reputation.

Mable did say that she had forgiven him, but there was nothing in her attitude and actions that would support her claim. During counseling, Mable's counselor talked to her about her unwillingness to forgive. The actual truth eventually came out: her belief that she lived alone her entire marriage and that God never intervened in the nightmare. Mable was hurt and felt it wasn't proportionally equitable to forgive after a year when she repeatedly suffered for two decades. The more sinister side of Mable believed that if she forgave Biff for his sin, it would be like he never sinned. From her perspective, he would get off free and clear, and the door of her nightmare would close as though it had never happened. That was not tenable for Mable. She was bitter and not ready to forget her hurt. In some ways, her hurt was a form of security. It was a reminder that kept her vigilant about what a person could do to her. She was like an institutionalized convict who couldn't live in any other place but the prison of unforgiveness.

Power of Unforgiveness

Biff indeed repented of his sin even though he did not initially confess it. Once it was in the open, he admitted everything. (See David's lack of confession until confronted by Nathan in 2 Samuel 12:1-12, Psalm 32:1-4, and Psalm 51:1-19). Mable was not impressed by his remorse and was unwilling to let him off the hook. She knew enough about God and the gospel to realize that forgiving someone was like saying,

I will obey God and forgive you for your sin regardless of what you have done to me. Because the power of forgiveness neutralizes sin, we will work on the damage done. I realize that what I have done to my Savior is far worse than what you have done to me or could ever do to me, even though what you have done to me has been devastating. Nevertheless, I will not hold this over your head any longer, but I will make myself vulnerable to the Lord, knowing that you could hurt me again. In essence, I trust God's sovereign care over my life and His method of conflict resolution rather than my own. I choose to be obedient to Him. I forgive you.

Her unwillingness to forgive Biff was a common-sense, human-centered way of protecting herself—an understandable temptation (1 Corinthians 1:25). Though she would not say it, Mable believed she would not be vulnerable as long as she could hold Biff's sin over his head. She was not grasping how her unforgiveness was forcing her head under the waters of bitterness. The power of the gospel is freely extending forgiveness to offenders either transactionally or attitudinally. The power of unforgiveness is choosing not to release yourself—attitudinally—or the other person—transactionally—from what happened. Mable essentially was saying that since God did not come through for her for twenty years, she would take matters into her hands. Her self-protective shield of unforgiveness was an attempt to accomplish three things:

- She was punishing Biff for all the years he punished her.
- She was protecting herself from ever being hurt again. (Of course, she was not protecting herself at all.)
- She was perverting the gospel.

Power of the Gospel

Sin disorients and distorts our thinking. Sin does not let God be God but entices us to assume the role of god-ness. Mable was playing god. She was holding Biff's sin over his head while mocking the cross. The Father's punishment of His Son on the cross was insufficient for Mable. While genuinely believing the gospel, she could not fully embrace its cleansing and freeing power. Grace seemed too easy. What Mable did not understand fully is that grace has never been effortless. For her to have the grace to forgive, it cost Jesus Christ His life. The infinite Father punished the Son for an infinite crime. The Savior paid an infinite price for the infinite crime. Biff and Mable received infinite forgiveness for their infinite crimes. Mable was unwilling to accept the death of Christ as a sufficient payment to cover Biff's sins.

She was treating her husband in a way that God did not treat her when she asked for forgiveness for the crimes she committed against Him. The irony in this story is that Biff is free as he walks out repentance, but Mable is in prison. Forgiving Biff does not say that what he did to her does not matter. It also does not let him off the hook because Biff needs help. Sin had captured him for many years (Galatians 6:1-3), and temptation continues to lure him into sin. If Mable wants to keep from being hurt again, she must work to do it God's way and forgive him. Being Biff's enemy worsens matters, complicating his temptation, their marriage, and her soul. Forgiving Biff will release both of them from what has been hindering them while positioning them to begin the process of actual restoration.

Call to Action

1. Who has hurt you? What did they do? What do you think about them? Are you free from what they did, or do you continue to harbor a sinful attitude toward them?
2. Are you holding onto any unforgiveness toward anyone? If so, what does unforgiveness reveal about your understanding of the gospel?
3. Will you talk about the irony of an offending person being free from their sin, but the victim of their sin continues to harbor sin because of what happened to them?
4. Do you see how unforgiveness hinders receiving the help the offended needs and hinders the offender's need to mature in Christ?
5. If you're hurting from what someone did to you, will you find help today to begin walking through any unwillingness to forgive—either attitudinally or transactionally—the person who hurt you?

5

Pre-forgiveness

Have you ever granted forgiveness to someone who hurt you? Did you mean it? Did you really, really mean it? Or did you say, "I forgive you," because it is the Christian thing to do? I'm not asking you this question with a cynical eye. I'm asking because I know from personal experience that there are times we can mouth the words "I forgive you," but the heart can be far from genuine. We can succumb to Christian speak to smooth over the situation, but our internal logic says we have more heart work to do to be right with God and the person we supposedly forgave.

Forgiveness Illustrated

Perhaps taking my little test on genuine forgiveness will help. After you forgave the person, were you able to talk about the hurt in such a way that communicated you were no longer managed by those hurts—whether you were speaking with God, yourself, or the offender? A sign of complete biblical forgiveness is when you can be offended, grant forgiveness, and talk about what happened to you without being controlled by the actions of those who hurt you. Though granting forgiveness can be a better version of how our culture works through their relational problems, it can be no more effective if the forgiveness is incomplete. A struggle to be genuine with the offender does not mean your forgiveness granting was not real, but it could mean your forgiveness is incomplete if you cannot genuinely let it go.

> As for you, you meant evil against me, but God meant it for good, to bring it about that many people should be kept alive, as they are today.
> (Genesis 50:20)

The speaker in this verse is Joseph, the son of Jacob. He is talking to his brothers, who initially tried to kill him but changed their collective minds and sold him to a ragtag group of slave traders. Joseph spent thirteen mostly horrible years away from his family while being accused of a crime he did not commit, which landed him in jail. During jail time, he was betrayed by those who could help him. It's hard to understand what happened to Joseph. Any of those incidents during his thirteen years would be enough to ruin his thoughts about God and life for the rest of his life. When we break into the story at Genesis 50:20, he finally has a chance to let his brothers know what he thought about their transgressions toward him. After thirteen astonishing years, Joseph has his first opportunity to face the instigators of his hardships. His response was forgiveness. Amazing grace. Joseph was ready for the moment. The Lord prepared his heart to grant the long overdue forgiveness to his persecutors.

What Is Pre-forgiveness?

In this story, we don't see the prerequisite heart work necessary for Joseph to be willing, gracious, and genuine to forgive his offenders. Before he could do business with his brothers, he had to do business with God. Missing this essential step in forgiveness means missing the opportunity to go the distance with someone who needs your forgiveness. This step is crucial because it gives you time to perceive the Lord's thoughts—as much as His thoughts can be ascertained—about what happened to you (Isaiah 55:8-9). You must reasonably establish a theologically precise understanding of God in your mind while convinced He is working good (Romans 8:28) in your life—even if it is in ways you did not expect or have not perceived up to this point in your journey. This process of forgiveness is the prerequisite work of pre-forgiveness.

When bad things happen to me, I can only process and accept them correctly after I have gained sovereign clarity on my troubles. Joseph had sovereign clarity. Do you have sovereign clarity on the disappointments in your life? When you review the movie of your life, can you see it with sovereign intentions? Suppose you cannot trust God's good work on your behalf. In that case, you will be a candidate for harboring bitterness, anger, anxiety, discouragement, criticism, resentment, cynicism, and even hate toward those who have hurt you. Not anchored by God's sovereign care of your life will make you like a kite in the wind. The Lord must be your anchor point as sin angles to capture you. Here are a few ways sin tries to snare its prey after someone does a dastardly deed to them.

- Our emotions enslave us as we continue to dwell on the offending person's actions.
- Our thoughts fixate on the hurt and what the person did to us.
- We struggle to process the nature of our relationship with the person.
- Our attitude toward the offender ensnares us.
- There is a relational awkwardness between us and the offender.
- Our hearts swirl in fluctuating desires as we try to gain clarity from the Lord.

Pre-forgiveness Illustrated

Mable's husband committed adultery. It was the most devastating news of her life. It took many months of biblical care, among many friends, in the context of her local church to help her walk through the crushing anguish of her heart. She called it her nightmare from Hades. When Biff repented, he eventually returned to Mable to ask for her forgiveness. His forgiveness was genuine; God changed Biff's heart. What he did not know is that Mable had already done business with God. She was ready to grant forgiveness. Her brand of forgiveness was more than her Christian duty. It was a God-centered, grace-empowered, gospel-motivated forgiveness. Mable was like Joseph. When the time came for forgiveness, the hard work of pre-forgiveness was over, and she was willing to grant genuine forgiveness.

The incredible power of the gospel was working in her heart. Mable had prayed for nearly fifteen years that God would transform their marriage. They had sex while dating, and though she never felt right about marrying Biff, it seemed like a better option than staying single. Mable was lonely. After their marriage, she became lonelier. Because of Biff's ongoing bouts of anger, their three sons rebelled against God. Biff and Mable were also struggling financially. They professed to be Christians though their church commitment was nominal. In God's autonomous and non-manipulatable timeframe, He answered Mable's fifteen-year prayer request to fix her marriage.

What did He do? He blew it up. God dropped a bomb in the middle of their marriage and blew it to smithereens. It's impossible to adequately describe the devastation on Mable and the children, especially if you have not lived it. From all perspectives, it made no sense. To find good or God in their mess was an incredible leap in human logic (1 Corinthians 1:25). As the numbness began to wear off, Mable began to seek God's thoughts on what was happening in her life, marriage, and family. That was when she came to the story of Joseph. Mable learned that God not only worked in the present, but He planned for the future.

Living in God's Story

Joseph and his family could not know that there would be a famine in the land, and the sovereign Lord needed someone in Egypt to set up things so that He could preserve the nation of Israel. As you know, God was not just doing this for the nation of Israel or Joseph's family. He did this because of His promise to Adam (Genesis 3:15) and Abraham (Genesis 12:1-3). Humanity needed a Savior (Galatians 4:4), and that Savior would come through Jacob's lineage. The bomb the good Lord dropped on Jacob's family flung Joseph to Egypt. According to God's predetermined plan, He scripted bad things into Joseph's life. Tossed in the crucible of suffering is what Joseph and Mable believed the Lord was up to with them, which motivated them to give up trying to control their respective stories while humbly stepping into God's story.

Joseph and Mable had sovereign clarity. It did not mitigate the pain or the dysfunction, but it did give them hope. After they had come to that place in their understanding, they were ready to move forward with God's new plans for their lives. The situation became less about what was happening to them and more about what God was doing through them. When you think through your disappointments, are you more aware of and affected by what God is doing, or are you more aware of and impacted by who did what to you? Can you humbly let go of the narrative you have been holding to and grasp the script God is writing for you? Perhaps you can do as Joseph did as he shared three things with his brothers:

- What God did was for good.
- What they did was evil.
- God's good triumphed over their evil.

Therefore, he could forgive his brothers for what they did to him. What controls your heart: what God allowed or what the offender did? Where do you put the accent mark: on the good of God or the evil of a person? How you answer those questions will determine the depth and quality of your forgiveness. If you cannot get to where Joseph was, you cannot release those who have sinned against you. One of the ways you can check your heart regarding your forgiveness of others for what they did to you is by how you think about what they did to you and how you talk about them. Proper thinking about personal suffering is where the gospel must have a more incredible grip on us than what others have done to us. One of the ways we can practicalize the gospel is how we perceive the offenses of others in light of our transgressions against the Lord.

Restoring Relationships

The cross of Christ has a way of downsizing the violations of others by giving me a proper perspective on my actions against God. If the same gospel that saved my soul cannot overcome the disappointment of others, the heart "gospelization" I need is not yet complete. Forgiveness flows out of a softened heart. The longer you stand before the Holy Lord you offended, the better it will go for you when you stand before the one who offended you. If you have done this well, you are in an excellent place to forgive the person who hurt you. The power of the gospel makes forgiveness real and practical.

Forgiveness is typically not the most challenging aspect if you have wrestled through pre-forgiveness. Note how Joseph was ready to forgive his brothers. He had thirteen years to figure this out with the Lord. I am not suggesting you need thirteen years to figure it out, but you must understand this concept—no matter how long it takes. If you do the hard work of pre-forgiveness, it will not be as difficult when the time comes for forgiveness. However, if it is hard, you must spend more time before the Lord because some residual anger toward Him and others is likely operating in your heart. We are all sovereigntists. Whether we consciously think about it or not, we all know that there is a God who ultimately controls everything. We call Him Jehovah.

Therefore, if you cannot forgive others for what happened to you, you must resolve the underlying issue between you and God first. Once you have sovereign clarity and can freely forgive the person who hurt you, you can go beyond the hurt by genuinely reconciling with the offender. Freedom to forgive is the best part, but it gets better. When Lucia and I make up in the way I have described here, we begin discussing the sin that separated us. The evil that enslaved us is now serving us. The sin becomes a practical working illustration we can talk about to grow and mature to the point where we reduce the amount of future sinning against each other. It should not be difficult to speak of sin if the power of the gospel has neutralized it. Killing it is vital because revisiting our past sins in non-punitive ways is essential to learn from our mistakes.

Call to Action

Here is the biblical linkage to maturity in a meaningful relationship:

1. **Pre-forgiveness:** When you allow God to adjust your heart so you can forgive.
2. **Forgiveness:** When you genuinely grant forgiveness to someone who hurt you.
3. **Reconciling:** When sin no longer separates you from the other person.
4. **Maturing:** After you neutralize the sin, you can discuss it with the hope that you don't do it again.

Just as Joseph could talk to his brothers non-punitively about what they did to him, you should be able to have similar discussions with your friends who sin against you. God answered Mable's prayer by blowing up her marriage, and she had enough sovereign clarity to accept and respond to her marital disappointment. That was seven years ago. The God-glorifying marriage she and Biff have today has swallowed those dark days, transforming them into a gospel tapestry. Though she was the one who was offended, she had a significant role to play in the restoration of her marriage. It began with the preparatory work in her heart. She was ready to forgive.

1. Has someone sinned against you? What did they do? How do you believe God intends to bring glory to Himself and restoration of the offender with you?
2. Are you able to forgive if they were to ask for your forgiveness? If not, you want to think through and apply what you have read to prepare your heart to forgive attitudinally or transactionally.
3. If you are ready to humbly forgive, whether they ever ask you to forgive them, you are free from their sin. There will be some situations where the offender does not seek forgiveness, but that should not hinder you from having a heart of forgiveness, freeing you from the offenses whether they are ever free.

6

How Many Times

Forgiveness is only one aspect of the change process. Forgiveness is not a complete change because there are several links—after forgiveness—in the repentance sequence. However, forgiveness is a vital mile marker that leads to full repentance, making this step nonnegotiable because we cannot experience ongoing transformation without biblically forgiving each other. But what if a person keeps asking for forgiveness and never changes? What are we to do with repeat offenders?

How Many Times?

> Then Peter came up and said to him, "Lord, how often will my brother sin against me, and I forgive him? As many as seven times?" Jesus said to him, "I do not say to you seven times, but seventy-seven times."
>
> (Matthew 18:21–22)

Peter raises a good question when he thought about the complexity of forgiveness: how often should we forgive the unchanging person? Jesus answered his question hyperbolically, pointing to our infinite opportunities to forgive offenders. The implication is clear: we must forgive those who genuinely ask, but it does not mean the asking person will change. If you have ever been in this spot with an offender, you know how forgiveness can wear thin if the offending person continues to behave poorly. Has someone in your life asked for forgiveness repeatedly but never changed their behavior?

Perhaps that person is you (Matthew 7:3–5). I know it's me. That's where my mind tends to go when I hear a question like what Peter asked. I know you don't want to be that person who always asks for forgiveness but never changes, but all of us are repeat offenders. What sinful habit continues to harass your soul? To still be stuck (Galatians 6:1) without ever changing can exasperate any relationship while testing the boundaries of Jesus' expectation for forgiveness—to forgive repeatedly. To live well with others requires more than a never-ending cycle of granting and receiving forgiveness, but what if they do not change?

He Never Changes

Put off your old self, which belongs to your former manner of life and is corrupt through deceitful desires, and to be renewed in the spirit of your minds, and to put on the new self, created after the likeness of God in true righteousness and holiness.
(Ephesians 4:22–24)

Biffy is twelve years old. His parents love the Lord and have tried to live that out in their home authentically. Emulating Jesus to Biffy has been their regular habituation on how to change, or what the Bible calls repentance. Paul's language in Ephesians 4:22–24 gives us a quick at-a-glance overview of total repentance with his put off, renew, and put on formula. Every believer brings an old way of living into their new walk with Jesus. Paul knew that. Thus, he gave the body of Christ a template for a total makeover. Christians have the privilege of working out their salvation (Philippians 2:12–13) progressively and incrementally, removing their former manner of thinking and behaving from their lives (James 1:22). Forgiveness is part of this comprehensive process.

Biffy knew this. His dad and mom have modeled and taught him well, and Biffy is not a flippant kid. He wants to do what is right. He has a heart for God (Acts 13:22), so he asks God to forgive him after he makes a mistake. He also asks his dad and mom for forgiveness if the offense is against either of them. But there is a problem: Biffy never changes. The never-changing person, who asks for forgiveness, is a test of the offended person's Christian maturity because a person's lack of change does not remove the responsibility of the offended person to forgive. God is our best example when it comes to forgiving repeat offenders. He will do it whenever we ask Him (1 John 1:9).

With an imitate-able God as our example (Ephesians 5:1), all Christians should be ready and willing to forgive someone when they ask them to do so. But let's press the point further. Even if they do not ask, we should be willing to appropriate God's free grace to forgive the person in our hearts. Their lack of asking should not be a reason for us to be under the control of their sinful actions. This mercy is the power of the gospel activated in our souls (Romans 1:16). Forgiveness—transactional or attitudinal—is our best option when someone offends us. Attitudinal forgiveness can always happen, even when the offender never pursues transactional forgiveness. "And Jesus said, 'Father, forgive them, for they know not what they do'" (Luke 23:34).

Beyond Forgiveness

Living in a relationship where nobody ever asks for forgiveness, or where someone does ask but change never occurs, can be hard enough. But if we use their lack of change as an excuse to hold on to our unforgiveness, we will make the problems worse by being captivated by their sin. The quicker we can appropriate God's grace with—at least—an attitude of forgiveness, the faster we will experience freedom from what happened to us regardless of what they do. Granted, some sins against us will be more challenging than others, but there is grace for that. An attitude of forgiveness frees us from what happened and prepares us to transact if the offender ever comes to us for forgiveness.

Biffy's willingness to seek forgiveness places him in the top 10 percent of the Christian class. And true to form, his parents tell him each time he requests their forgiveness how glad they are to release him from what he did (Romans 2:4). On several occasions, a parent has taken the time to walk him through the necessity of not just being released from the guilt of his actions but for him to push beyond forgiveness toward repentance. They want him to fully repent to be uncaught from the repeated patterns of sin in his life (Galatians 6:1-2). An example of this is if you choose to be angry at someone, it would be wise and humble to seek forgiveness. It would be better to break the habituated patterns of anger that have captivated your soul (2 Corinthians 10:3-6; James 4:1-3). Reflecting on my years of counseling with families, I have observed three recurring themes of forgiveness and repentance practices in Christian homes.

1. Forgiveness and repentance have not been part of their family dynamic.
2. Forgiveness and repentance have been partial but not complete in their homes.
3. Forgiveness and repentance have been entirely and consistently employed within the family.

No Repentance

This kind of family has no repentance language operative in their homes. Things like sin, guilt, conviction, confession, forgiveness, and reconciliation are not part of their daily vocabulary. Occasionally, an "I'm sorry" will be tossed about for mitigating relational tension but not for genuinely owning an offense or transforming a relationship. Perhaps they have not been discipled well. Maybe these Christians are part of a local church that does not practice complete repentance. It could be there is no humility, the prerequisite to God's grace. The Lord's empowering favor is negated because of His resistance toward proud hearts (James 4:6; Romans 1:18).

For many, it's a bad habit never illuminated by the Spirit or addressed within their closest relationships. I can testify to this. For the first five years of our marriage, I never asked my wife to forgive me for anything. I never changed in any meaningful long-term ways as far as our one-flesh union was concerned. We were shuffling and stumbling toward a business partner relationship or roommate status. Mercifully, the Lord imposed Himself on our marriage. We began the long, tedious, and arduous process of practicing repentance in our relationship, which has become a daily habit (Galatians 2:20). There is no doubt in our minds that what I'm sharing with you was the means of grace that transformed us and our marriage.

Partial Repentance

The second group of Christians employs the forgiveness language but does not have a transparent, practical, working model of complete repentance. Though they are a notch higher than the "I'm sorry" crowd, the kudos stop there because of their similarity to the "I'm sorry" crowd. There is no adequate, sustained transformation in their lives. They have roller-coaster seasons of getting along and seasons of struggle. They can be mainly civil to each other, especially because they have learned to get along in public. But the gospel's transformative power is not dramatically and dynamically empowered in their homes. They experience small changes because they are growing old together, and there is some residual effect from being in a Bible-teaching church. We can do better.

When the power of the Word of God and the Spirit of God come alive in humble hearts and lives, families experience transformation. Change is the power of the gospel, awakening dark and dull hearts (Hebrews 5:12–14). Maybe the most common reason for a partially repentant home is because one spouse is unwilling to change for whatever reason. A wife who resists her husband's biblical attempts to lead her will cause any marriage to flounder. This grieving (Ephesians 4:30) or quenching (1 Thessalonians 5:19) what God can do for them will always keep their marriage from what it should be (Ephesians 5:31–32).

Complete Repentance

The third kind of family is a confessing and forgiving one that is intentional about helping each other change. When sin happens, they own it. That's called confession. Then forgiveness is asked for and granted, which is only the beginning of the change process. So many grace-empowered opportunities await this kind of family that lives out repentance. After they neutralize the sin through gospel forgiveness, they move to the glorious step of genuinely reconciling with each other. That's when you can have an unencumbered gospel group hug. The power of Jesus removes the wall of hostility (Ephesians 2:14).

The offender and the offended are now partners in the transformative gospel (Philippians 1:5). They are for each other, which is one of the core tenets of the gospel practicalized (Romans 8:31). They prove this attitude repeatedly by engaging each other after they forgive each other to become educated about what went wrong. They want to help each other mortify (Romans 8:13) and amputate (Matthew 5:30) all bad attitudes, words, and actions, which is the power of the gospel activated in them. You will know if the power of the gospel has successfully neutralized the sin between you and another person by how you both talk about what went wrong after you have reconciled.

If the forgiveness exchange was authentic, there is no reason for two people—in an ongoing relationship—to keep from talking about what went wrong. To miss out on this essential discussion is to miss out on an opportunity to help someone change (Galatians 6:1-2). Discussing the sin between two people without judgment is a real sign that the gospel has rendered the offense dead. It also helps to keep the offender from becoming a repeat offender, which is what was going on with Biffy. A few characteristics of this kind of gospelized family are openness, transparency, honesty, and humility, plus an intentional willingness to serve in the sanctification of the entire family (Hebrews 10:24). You'll also observe relational warmth, kindness, and genuineness in their communication (Ephesians 4:29-32).

Call to Action

1. Are you in a relationship where someone is a repeat offender? It's a trick question; you are a repeat offender, and so am I. Nobody is perfect. Everybody has problems that have become patterns. Therefore, the better question should center around your recurring bad habits. With you in view, do you regularly push past forgiveness by seeking to change? If so, great!
2. What is one of your habitual sin patterns? As you think about that pattern in your life, would you characterize yourself as a full repenter? I realize you may not have gained a complete victory over that sin, but have you formed the habits found in the order of repentance: confession, forgiveness, reconciliation, and restoration?
3. Do your primary relationships practice complete repentance? If not, what are some things that keep you all from having gospel-transforming relationships?
4. I gave some characteristics of a repenting home: openness, transparency, honesty, humility, and relational warmth toward each other. How would you characterize your family relationships? In what ways are you willing to change?

7

Un-asking Spouse

Mable came to me, exclaiming, "I'm frustrated! I am always approaching my husband with my sin, asking for his forgiveness, but he seems never to see his need to ask me for forgiveness. Many times he won't even bother to forgive me. What am I to do? How can I respond to him when he shows no interest in working with me through our problems?" Her complaint is not unusual in relationships, married or otherwise. Her situation is probably the norm because folks do not mature equally or at the same pace. Let me share with you what I told her, and, of course, you can apply these things to either gender, not just Biff.

Inequitable Relationships

There is always a smell of death to our most complicated questions because to walk well with God in His world, there is a call to die to ourselves (Mark 8:34). How could it be any other way? Living among the walking dead is not always complicated in some areas of our lives, but it can be pretty challenging in other situations. When there is sin, there will be ancillary problems that need our utmost care. Most of the tight spots where dying to yourself is hard are in our most meaningful relationships.

Part of the problem will always be relationship inequity; everybody is in a different place. Each person has a unique way of seeing things and responding to them. For example, parenting is a testing grounds where one child progresses well while the other does not. Marriage is another testing ground where being different can cause conflict. Thinking biblically about our differences while learning to respond like Jesus to those not like us is worth our consideration.

Let me provide you with three ideas I told Mable, and then I will add four other tips that I hoped would help her to reflect Christ to Biff (1 Peter 3:1-2). I do not assume you are married or that your situation is like hers, so if it serves you, please change and adapt what you need to so that these concepts will aid you in your most vital relationships. Perhaps you are Biff, and it's Mable who is stubborn or oblivious about the needs of the marriage. If that is the case, make those adjustments while asking God to provide you the wisdom and courage to be Jesus to her.

Is He Illuminated?

While I'm sure you've considered the condition of Biff's soul, I would like you to consider why he did not ask you for forgiveness. Perhaps you live in a Christianized community or are part of a church where it's not unusual to mimic religious behaviors. What do you think his lack of asking means? There can be a difference between doing Christian things and being a Christian (James 1:22; Philippians 2:12-13). If he is not a Christian, there is no way he can ask you for forgiveness that will be adequate, consistent, or transformative (1 Corinthians 2:14). To know you've sinned and to be motivated to remove your sin is a Spirit-led, Spirit-illuminated, and Spirit-empowered gift (John 16:13; 1 John 1:7-10).

Even a non-Christian can premeditate and act out choreographed responses that look like a believer if he has time to think, plan, and implement Christianized responses. With enough runway, he can control his words, actions, and reputation. Thus, there are two crucial areas to consider when thinking about whether he is a Christian: those spontaneous moments in his life where he's caught by surprise and how he lives when nobody is looking.

During surprise moments, we must reflex quickly without considering how we might look to others. These unannounced instances do not matter to the Christian because he can keep in step with the Spirit and be under the Spirit's management each moment of the day (Galatians 5:16). Nobody ever caught Jesus off guard. He was under the influence of the Spirit rather than fleshly desires (Romans 8:6). Secondly, there is a difference between our public and private lives. We are tempted to let down our guards when the world is not watching. There is no craving for favorable opinions or fears of rejection. We relax. We live in harmony with who we really are.

- How do you know he is a Christian?
- What is he like in those private moments when it's just you and him?
- How does he respond when surprised? What are some of the first things that come out of his mouth?
- What are his sensitivity levels of morality? Has his conscience been growing harder or softer throughout your marriage?

Is He Ignorant?

The Ethiopian in Philip's day did not understand God's Word (Acts 8:31). He needed guidance (John 17:17). The Bible speaks about the value of teachers (Ephesians 4:12-14; James 3:1), and Philip was one to this man. We can't know what we don't know. Maybe the light of the Spirit is turned on, but Biff does not know how to repent, or nobody ever taught him the importance of confession and forgiveness (2 Timothy 3:16-17). Practicing the skill of repentance is not universally understood within the Christian community.

For example, Christians regularly say unkind things to each other on social media while never returning to ask for forgiveness. Thirty minutes on any social media platform would support this claim. I have discovered that most Christian couples I have counseled do not know how to practice repentance. When I ask them to walk me through what repentance looks like in their marriages, nearly all return blank stares or stumble through some apology process with no redemptive force.

- Will he say, "I'm sorry," for things he does wrong and leave it at that?
- Does he know how to ask for forgiveness?
- Has he ever asked someone else to forgive him?
- Can he walk you through the process of repentance?

Is He Insecure?

Fear of others is real (Proverbs 29:25). It is most challenging around people we know best, those with whom the need for vulnerability is more challenging. It is easier to be transparent and honest with strangers. People we may never see again are typically risk-free relationships. Online communities are like this so that a person might be freer to communicate more in a community like a social media platform than with in-person relationships. Shame, guilt, vulnerability, honesty, and transparency are part of the human complexity that needs constant mortification to have redemptive relationships (Romans 8:13).

Men may appear to have a tougher-looking facade, and they may know how to present hardness, aloofness, or having it all together, but we're all weak clay jars (Genesis 2:7; 2 Corinthians 4:7). Eve did not get more shame, guilt, and fear than Adam. Sin came upon all people equally and without measure (Romans 3:23, 5:12). Adam has penetrated, permeated, and perplexed your husband's inner person. It could be that he knows what to do, but his high estimation of himself keeps him from lowering himself to a place where he can humbly ask for your forgiveness.

- In what ways have you observed his insecurity?
- How does he appear stronger, more fabulous, or better than others?
- How does he think about and guard his reputation?
- What areas have you seen where he has been humble, open, and vulnerable?

Are You Doing What You Can?

> *If possible, so far as it depends on you, live peaceably with all.*
>
> (Romans 12:18)

I call Paul's appeal to do our part the 50 percent verse. He asks us to do everything we can and what is biblically expected regarding conflict resolution. You can't do everything for your husband and should not, but you must do as much as it depends on you. Reaching out to others is one of those things that can be helpful when stuck in a relational conflict. Don't hold back from seeking help. God did not intend our journey to be isolated (Genesis 2:18).

If you have followed Matthew's template for restoring someone (Matthew 18:15-17) and he is not changing, pray about where you can find help. No wife is biblically bound to submit to a sinful husband in every way. God has not called you to be a doormat to him, nor has He called you to be his authority. You're co-laborers, presumably spiritual brother and sister. Unbiblical submission or authority does not leave you without options. You may need to go outside his authority to find another biblical authority to help your marriage.

- Are you doing all you can?
- How do you know?
- What hinders you from seeking outside help?
- Do you have a close friend who can offer wise and courageous biblical perspectives about you?

Are You Assessing Yourself?

The saying is trustworthy and deserving of full acceptance that Christ Jesus came into the world to save sinners, of whom I am the foremost.
(1 Timothy 1:15)

A sober self-assessment of all the aspects of your life is essential when thinking about helping difficult people (Galatians 6:1–2). Paul never got over the fact of his total depravity. Though he did not wallow in his depravity by practicing a woe-is-me mindset, there was no inhibition in reminding himself of what he used to be. You hear this in his language to the Corinthians. He carried them in his heart as he continually thanked God for them.

Though they may have been the most difficult Christians in his life, you can feel his love for them. (Read 1 Corinthians 1:1–9.) That attitude is what you want for your husband. I know he has sinned against you, but there is a more significant issue in play—he put Christ on the cross, which is the ground-leveling truth, and so did you. The cross of Christ is the human equalizer where all badness (and goodness—Isaiah 64:6) means nothing compared to what we did to Christ.

- How does your attitude objectively and daily reflect that you are for your husband?
- From your perspective, do you consider him a bigger sinner? (Your day-to-day thoughts, attitudes, words, and behaviors are where you'll find the answer to this question.)

- Describe your prayers for him. Does he feel your affection for him?
- Does Christ's work in your life have more control over you than your husband's behaviors?

Are You Practicing God's Kindness?

Or do you presume on the riches of his kindness and forbearance and patience, not knowing that God's kindness is meant to lead you to repentance?
(Romans 2:4)

God gave us what we did not deserve. Rather than heaping wrath on our lives (Romans 1:18), the good Lord motivated us to change by His kindness. Mercy drew us out of darkness (Psalm 34:6). The Lord heaped riches upon riches on us, and He has not stopped since the first time we repented (Romans 10:9, 13). Paul gives us a short list of God's riches that He employs to help people change: kindness, forbearance, and patience. Read 1 Corinthians 13:4–7 and Galatians 5:22–23 for a few more.

God desires to encourage us rather than critique us to the point of deflation. I have already made a case for identifying your husband's problems and asked you to find outside help. The issue I have in view here is not finding fault in him but being a means of grace that encourages him toward change, which is why one of my earlier questions was about whether or not you're for him. You should overlook his sin as much as you can.

- What does he experience the most from you—your encouragement or discouragement?
- Are you quicker to see what he does wrong or right?
- When was the last time you encouraged him? Explicitly, what did you say to him?

- Have you gossiped about him or said any other unkind thing to others about him?

Are You Waiting For the Gift?

And the Lord's servant must not be quarrelsome but kind to everyone, able to teach, patiently enduring evil, correcting his opponents with gentleness. God may grant them repentance leading to a knowledge of the truth.

(2 Timothy 2:24–25)

I have occasionally thought about what it would be like to have the ability to make people change, but I always come back to the wisdom in accepting my finitude. The power of repentance needs to rest in the hands of someone a bit more omniscient than I am, and more loving too. At times I fail in knowledge and love. Though I'm okay with being unable to grant repentance, I struggle with submitting my expectations about others to God. Specifically, when I expect people to be a certain way and they do not meet my expectations, my response at that moment will tell you what controls me.

Whatever controls you will be your functional god. Jesus tied our hearts to our treasures in Matthew 6:21. One of the most effective ways to find out what your treasure is will come in the moments of your disappointments, especially your recurring ones. When a lack of change in someone conflicts with your desires for a better kind of response from them, you'll have to decide what will have the most power over you. That kind of tug-o-war of the heart was going on with Jesus in the garden of Gethsemane (Luke 22:24).

- Whose will has the most power over you? Your husband's? Yours? Or the Lord's?

- Do you know how to appropriate God's grace while awaiting His hopeful repentance?
- What things have you learned about your faith through this marriage disappointment?
- How are you fortifying your soul for the potential of a lack of change in your husband's life?

Call to Action

1. I have given you several questions to work through as you think about your spouse. Will you take all of them to the Lord and be brutally honest with Him? Afterward, will you share your thoughts and questions with a true friend while appealing to your friend to be compassionately and courageously frank?
2. Your opening statement was about frustration. While it would be great to categorize it as righteous anger, that would not be the whole truth. You cannot stay where you are. Your husband may never change, but you must. Perchance, he never changes; you need help so that your walk with Christ is not negatively affected by his lack of change. Talk to your friend about these things.

8

Manipulating Forgiveness

Biff asked, "As a believer, does God's Word require me to forgive a relative of mine time after time—essentially let her off the hook—for her unkind behavior and attitude toward me and the many cruel and untrue things she has done behind my back to other family members? She never asks for forgiveness and only tells me I need to understand her feelings. Am I wrong to stay my distance and set some boundaries?" What would you say to Biff? Have you ever had a situation like this with a friend or relative who was gaslighting you, tricking you to accommodate their sinfulness? How did you handle it?

Biff's Heart

Biff's question is multi-layered; I will try to answer it while adding a few other twists that some folks have grafted into the teaching about forgiveness, which Biff's relative may be doing. Of course, the first place to begin with biblical forgiveness is always with our hearts before we start figuring out what's happening with the other person. The go-to text when it comes to humble self-assessment is Matthew 7:3–5. The purpose of this passage is to help us carefully reconstruct biblical thinking, specifically how we think about ourselves before we engage others. If our first thought has something to do with the speck in their eye rather than our own timber, we need to start over by reorienting our minds to what Jesus is teaching in that text.

I like to say it this way: "No matter what someone has done to me, it does not compare with what I have done to my Lord." If that kind of soul-leveling, cross-exalting perspective is our point of departure, we will be free and clear to think more redemptively about the other person. This teaching is always imperative but typically intensifies when discussing forgiveness with relatives. With our hearts humbled by the gospel, our compassion for the troublesome relative is the next thing to assess. Our pity for a difficult person will be different from those who are easier to love, so it's essential we jump-start our hearts by keeping the cross in view so we're moving toward genuine compassion for them. If we don't do this, it would be wise to withhold our correction until our hearts experience gospel recalibrating.

Biff's Goal

As we continue to assess ourselves, we want to add Paul's teaching in Romans 12:18, where he said, "So far as it depends on you, live peaceably with all." We are on a peacemaking mission. That was the Lord's objective with us, to remove the hostility between Him and us so that we could experience reconciliation (Ephesians 2:14). A similar kind of Christlike example should be what we have in mind with our relatives and friends. We want to do everything we can to be at peace with them. As you know, the implication of Paul's teaching not only applies to us, but there is a requirement on them too, which means you might not be at peace with them if they do not do their part.

- Do you view yourself as the foremost sinner in all relationships as Paul considered himself (1 Timothy 1:15)?
- Do you hope to bring peace to a challenging relationship, as much as it depends on you (Romans 12:18)?

Biff's Method

> Or do you presume on the riches of his kindness and forbearance and patience, not knowing that God's kindness is meant to lead you to repentance?
> (Romans 2:4)

You could state Paul's question to the Romans this way: don't you know that the riches of God's kindness, forbearance, and patience lead to the change you hope for in your relatives and friends? He reminds us how God brought us to a place of change, which Biff hopes will happen to his relative as he cooperates with the Lord in that redemptive possibility. This God-centered, gospel-empowered approach is what we should be modeling and delivering to our stubborn and undeserving friends (Romans 5:8, 2:8–9).

However, a fair warning is that if you are kind and patient, they may not change. Either way, that outcome is not our responsibility (1 Corinthians 3:6). Our job is to do as much as depends on us while resting in the truth that we cannot provide repentance to anyone (2 Timothy 2:25). What we are responsible for is how we approach people. We are not biblically permitted to engage anyone with a sinful attitude. Jesus died on the cross, and we will have to die too, which is our best shot at cooperating with God in people's restoration.

1. **Heart:** You realize you have the log in your eye, and they have specks in theirs.

2. **GOAL:** You hope to be at peace with others–so far as it depends on you.
3. **METHOD:** Your approach looks like kindness, forbearance, and patience.

Sloppy Forgiveness

I addressed Biff's heart, goal, and method because I have seen too many times when Christians have confronted people without considering a careful pre-confrontation analysis of their hearts. As to Biff's question, I am not aware of any teaching in the Bible that appeals to us to release someone from their sin when they are not asking God—or any other offended person—for release from their sin. Forgiveness—asking, granting, and receiving—is the transactional process of letting a person's sin go after they ask for freedom from their sin. In a forgiveness context, the sinning person understands there is a debt that someone must pay (Romans 6:23).

This concept is a significant plank in the gospel platform: Christ died for our sins, and we must ask Him to forgive us to be free from our sins. A just God sets the standard. We agree with His standard, and when we cross the line of His standard (transgress), we ask Him to forgive us. We acknowledge our wrongs, which is our agreement (confession) with God while seeking forgiveness (justified) from Him (1 John 1:9). Forgiveness without God involved is not forgiveness at all. God is the only person who can release anyone from their sins, and He will not do this unless we ask Him through genuine repentance. Biff cannot release her.

That would be similar to a victim releasing the culprit of a crime, while the judge is never part of the process. The criminal must have her day in court. If she genuinely engaged God and He forgave her legally, I do not think she would be hiding, ignoring, or excusing her sin to Biff. That does not make biblical sense, and if God did forgive her, she would not only need to come to Biff so he could forgive her, but she would want to go to Biff—not for forensic cleansing, but for relational reconciliation.

Relational Manipulation

What Biff is describing is not biblical forgiveness but relational manipulation. Without God's forgiveness, it is the equivalent of Biff standing on a street corner waving a wand over folks as they pass by, releasing them from their sins. In such a scene, they could be forgiven for anything, regardless of whether they asked God for such mercy, and anyone could do it. They would not even have to know what Biff was doing for them. Freedom from sin without asking for it or knowing about it is sloppy theology. It renders the death of Christ meaningless.

If we could release people willy-nilly from their sins without going through the proper channels of atonement, there would be no need for Christ's life, death, and resurrection. Each of us is without excuse for our sins (Romans 1:20). We will be held accountable for our sins, and the only way we can experience release from them is by genuinely asking God to forgive us. How many times have you sinned against someone and asked them to forgive you but did not ask God to forgive you? I have done this a few times. While I can somewhat clear up the relational breakdown between another person and me, there is still an offense against God. All sin is against God, and there are no exceptions.

Biff's relative is in a more profound entanglement than she realizes, and this kind of biblical reasoning is the approach I recommend that Biff prays about until it's clear to him. Maybe the Lord will give her favor by releasing her captivated soul. Her problem has to do more with God than with Biff. She needs to have a clearer understanding of biblical forgiveness. Sometimes Christian people play the forgiveness card like a wild card in a game. They throw it down whenever they like to fix a problem. It becomes their get-out-of-jail-free card without doing the biblical heavy lifting with God. For some, it's a weak, non-sustainable attempt at relational damage control rather than redemptive freedom. Asking for forgiveness may sound better than an apology, but if it begins and ends with the offended human while never seeing the Divine Judge, it's forensic impotence.

How to Love Her

Granting forgiveness to a non-asking person is a grace mistake. Some call this extending grace, a way of being nice while not serving the person in sin's clutches (Galatians 6:1). Grace extenders do the gospel a disservice by muting its efficacy. Biff's relative is minimizing her sin while asking him to ignore it—to extend grace. That is dangerous. The question Biff will have to ask himself is whether he is the person who needs to bring her conniving ways to the light, which leads to his boundary question. I'm not fond of the standard connotation that some folks upload to the boundary idea.

In almost all cases, when a person talks about boundaries, they are not thinking redemptively about the other person. Rather than discussing borders, it would be better to frame the question this way: "What is the most effective way I can love her rather than the most effective way I can construct a wall between us?" She may rebuff a redemptive approach, leaving Biff with no other option but a need for rebuke, confrontation, and separating, which fit nicely within a redemptive worldview. If there are boundaries, Biff should let her set them after he pursues her redemptively.

Call to Action

Here are a few questions for Biff to take to the Lord. If you're in a similar spot, will you consider them too? Ask the Spirit to illuminate your mind by bringing you the answers you need for clarity and detail.

1. Do you consider yourself a bigger sinner than others? (An effective way to answer this question is by examining how you think and talk about others.)
2. Is your primary goal for troubling people is for them to have a great relationship with Christ? This objective should be your goal with every person, not just the easy-to-get-along-with people in your life.
3. If so, what are you doing that is helping or hindering this process?
4. Are you approaching others with a heart of kindness, forbearance, and patience? How do you need to talk to God about your heart toward others?
5. Are you the one who is in the best position to clean up a person's sloppy forgiveness worldview, which in the case of Biff's relative, she seems comfortable perpetuating?

Miscellany

Biff's relative reminds me of the rich young ruler (Mark 10:17–27). He came to Jesus, asking Him to justify and ignore his sin. Jesus was in the best position to respond to him. I would recommend that Biff prays about doing this for her. Like the rich young man, there is a good chance she will end the relationship, but he'll be redemptive, not boundary-setting. Let her determine how things will go. If his heart is right with God and the Lord has given Biff compassion for her, it would be unloving not to confront her.

What Biff has described about his relative is no different

from any relational situation where one person asks another person to ignore their sin. Does he love her enough to tell her the truth (Ephesians 4:15)? As you think about that question, consider two possible hindrances that could tempt us not to go forward in a loving confrontation.

- "If I confront her, will she reject me or become angry with me?"
- "If I confront her, will I lose the relationship?"

Forgiveness between two parties must be transactional, whether with God or another person. Both sides must be biblically engaged with each other, humbly seeking and granting forgiveness. There is a chance Biff's relative will never humbly and genuinely seek his forgiveness. If so, it will not be transactional, and she will not experience forgiveness. Still, his forgiveness can be attitudinal, which deals with his heart as he thinks about her. It also deals with how he relates to the Lord regarding his relative: she should not be a temptation for him to sin when thinking about her. Regardless of what she does, he can be free from her shenanigans in a similar way in which Jesus was free from sin when He thought about those who hurt Him (Luke 23:34). The real question is, "What depends on Biff regarding this relationship, and whatever that is, will he do it?" (See Romans 12:18; James 4:17.)

9

Lingering Unforgiveness

A pastor asked, "As a full-time elder and pastor for twenty-seven years, I have seen and walked with people through many forms of offenses and relational conflict. Your resources are helpful and needed in the church today. In the following scenario, I wonder if you could address forgiveness and the need to walk free from resentment and bitterness. I see so many folks who do not do forgiveness well, and when that happens, anger, resentment, and bitterness captivates them. How would you help a person like this? Let me share a case study with you."

Case Study

Once a pastor, Bert has been deeply offended and believes he has been stabbed in the back by someone he once cared for and mentored. He believes Biff gossiped, slandered, and convinced others to side with him to oust Bert from leadership in the church. Bert thinks Biff has lied to the church and others. He says Biff is a snake. Biff has legitimately sinned against Bert. Although he has confessed these offenses and agrees there were things he did wrong, Bert will not meet with him or forgive him until he agrees in writing and publicly owns all the sins committed, according to Bert's perspective.

Bert also believes his viewpoint is 100 percent accurate. Bert's sin list regarding Biff includes his motives, with which Biff disagrees. However, Biff is willing to meet and work toward reconciliation. Meanwhile, Bert is bitter, though he denies it. Bert has even cut off all interaction with certain people—including family members who have continued to attend the church, or those who have not taken a stance against Biff. Bert sees Biff as his enemy and anyone else who sides with him. He has justified his unforgiveness toward Biff to certain family members and will not relent until he fully repents according to his stipulations.

- Are we to forgive in our hearts or have pre-forgiveness for someone who does not see they're wrong, confess it correctly, or ask for forgiveness?
- What about an offended person who sets forth a list of offenses and a standard for repentance, confession, and forgiveness that the alleged offender can never meet?
- Is Bert justified in his heart of unforgiveness?
- Can the offended forgive from the heart without a full confession or repentance from the offender? Would that be pre-forgiveness?
- Will you touch on the distinction between forgiveness and trust in a relationship where someone has broken the trust?

What Is Pre-forgiveness?

Pre-forgiveness is a term I coined as I reflected on the story of Joseph from Genesis 37–50, mainly as I observed his interaction with his brothers in the book's final chapter. Joseph's attitude was Christlike toward his brothers. He did not show bitterness, unkindness, or unforgiveness toward them—even though they were not repentant or requesting his forgiveness. Pre-forgiveness is a heart of forgiveness before Joseph ever had an opportunity to forgive them transactionally. The implication here is that Joseph had spent time with the Lord and, in personal reflection, worked through the acute tragedies and disappointments that came at the hands of his brothers (Acts 2:23; Luke 23:34). By the time the opportunity for Joseph to grant forgiveness to his brothers, God had prepared his heart for transactional forgiveness.

I do not know how long Joseph's soul was free enough or out from under the control of his perpetrating brothers because the Bible does not say. What is clear is that Joseph was a free man even while in bondage in Egypt—the place his sinful brothers sent him. Though they were not free from their crimes, Joseph was free from them—in his heart. The question is whether or not a person should come to the place of pre-forgiveness like Joseph, which would show evidence of an attitude ready to forgive the offender per the offender's request. The answer is an absolute yes for three reasons:

- We should always be willing to forgive anyone regardless of their actions.
- Whether the offender asks or not, the desire to forgive keeps the offended from a captured heart.
- An attitude of forgiveness models Christlikeness.

Willing to Forgive

Being willing to forgive is not forgiving. A desire to forgive does not release the offender from his sin. To be free from sin, the offender must ask someone to release him from his transgression. Otherwise, you could forgive anyone you wanted, whether they knew it or not or asked for it. The idea of pre-forgiveness has very little to do with the offender. It is about the offended. It is an opportunity for the offended to keep from drowning in bitterness. Have you met that kind of person? A common occurrence is someone legitimately hurt, and the offender has not asked for forgiveness. All of us have been sinned against by people who have never asked for forgiveness. Offended people come in two kinds:

- Those who struggle with bitterness, criticalness, cynicism, suspicion, gossip, slander, unforgiveness, or anger.
- Those who are free from those temptations, even though the power of the gospel has not nullified the offender's sins.

> For this is a gracious thing, when, mindful of God, one endures sorrows while suffering unjustly. For what credit is it if, when you sin and are beaten for it, you endure? But if when you do good and suffer for it you endure, this is a gracious thing in the sight of God. For to this you have been called, because Christ also suffered for you, leaving you an example, so that you might follow in his steps.
>
> (1 Peter 2:19–25)

Humility, self-awareness, maturity, and contentment characterize this second group because they have learned to find peace in a fallen world. Jesus was the most impressive at doing this, and He is our example as we walk in His steps. We cannot satisfactorily resolve every sin. Thus, Christians must have a clear-headed, practical understanding and application of the gospel. They will be susceptible to all kinds of pitfalls if they do not.

- Who has sinned against you and has not come to you seeking your forgiveness?
- Is your heart more controlled by God's peace or others' sins?

- What must you do to have a heart of forgiveness—like Joseph—regardless of whether your offender has sought forgiveness?

Pre-scripting Forgiveness

Should Bert prescribe the depth and extent of Biff's forgiveness? That is an interesting question because the Lord did that for us. He specified how we are to repent and the conditions for our repentance but with a gospel-ironic twist: perfection. He set the standard for repentance so high that none of us could meet it. He did this purposefully so that we would avoid the temptation to rely on ourselves for rescue (legalism) but on His works as the only means for salvation (Ephesians 2:8-9). Therefore, you could say there is a precedent to what Bert is doing, but an example does not mandate a pattern.

I suspect many parents have scripted repentance with their children. The child sins, and the parent asks them to repent. Then they begrudgingly grunt out an "I'm sorry" under duress. It was precisely according to the parent's prescription, but what did the parent accomplish? Mandated repentance is not necessarily repentance. True repentance is when the offender experiences convincing by the Spirit of God, according to the Word of God, of the sins committed. He then tells the offended person the reason that he is seeking forgiveness. We call this confession—to agree with God (and others) about what he did.

We regularly ask each other about our offenses in our home so we can agree on what happened. That is typical Christian behavior. It requires the offender's and the offended's humility to concur with the sins committed. Any Christian offender should have enough self-suspicion to ask the offended for help to see the offense. Why not? If you were sick, you'd want a doctor's input so you could be free from what was ailing you. It is an act of humility born out of a sober self-awareness that self-deception is real. However, asking the offended for his perspective does not automatically mean complete agreement with their assessment.

Spirit-led Cooperation

After collecting all the data, the Spirit of God convinces the offender of the offenses, which is the Spirit's work, not hurt-centered, man-centered manipulations. Bert is not justified in holding on to a heart of unforgiveness. To be justified is to be declared not guilty. Justification is a courtroom term where the judge declares someone guilty or not guilty. If the judge slams the gavel down and says, "Not guilty," the person is justified. Only God determines actual guilt. Thus, the question is about Bert's justification for holding a strict protocol for forgiveness. The best answer is yes and no. He is partially correct in that Biff did some things wrong.

Of course, Biff has admitted (confessed) that he had sinned against Bert while owning his need for forgiveness. Thus, Bert is right (justified) and should grant forgiveness if Biff asks him. However, it appears that Bert has not stewarded his forgiveness problem biblically. He does not have the attitude of Christ regarding those who have sinned against him (Luke 23:34). He is hurt, which you would expect, so you don't want to judge him uncharitably, but he has not submitted his hurt to the power of Christ, as Peter instructed us about walking in the steps of Jesus. Peter continued, saying,

> When he was reviled, he did not revile in return; when he suffered, he did not threaten, but continued entrusting himself to him who judges justly.
> (1 Peter 2:23)

Though it would be nice if all offenders sought to make amends with all offended people, it is unrealistic to hold to such an unreasonable expectation. To do so is a temptation to anger or despair. We must deal with this reality in our fallen world, one of the more remarkable things about the gospel. Christ loved me while I was sinning (Romans 5:8). He would never let me off the hook until I humbled myself before Him and asked for His mercy. Stunningly, even though Christ held my sins against me, He loved me to death. If that kind of gospel expectation (and privilege) does not change and control our hearts, the power of our offenders will always hold us down.

Wisdom Issues

Let's suppose Bert and Biff could legitimately experience forgiveness by the power of the gospel. God neutralizes all the sins committed between them. The question then centers on whether their future relationship could function as a trusted one as though there was no sin between them. In most situations like this, it is possible. For example, my wife and I sin against each other occasionally, and we trust, love, and adore each other. Then there are other relationships where having that level of access and intimacy is impossible. Sexual offenses come to mind.

If someone sexually abused one of our daughters and by some extraordinary act of the grace of God, there was forgiveness requested and granted, I would do all I could to keep the forgiven abuser from our daughters. Forgiveness of sin does not necessarily mean the removal of future wrongdoing. The doctrine of progressive sanctification informs us that we will never experience sinless perfection in the here and now. Though a person receives forgiveness, it does not mean they will never commit that sin again. It would be cruel to suggest the offender and the offended pursue an ongoing relationship in a situation such as sexual abuse.

The lack of ongoing relationships is a sad consequence of our fallenness. I am not saying this should be the case between Bert and Biff. But it appears that Bert is not interested in reconciliation at this time. It seems like the best hope for reconciliation would be third-party intervention to help Bert come to a more reasonable attitude and response. Sin hurts deeply. We know this. I am sure Bert is hurting deeply, and though forgiveness is the proper response, it may take him a while to come to that place in his heart. I would ask the Spirit of God to bring restorative care to his soul, hoping for future reconciliation.

Call to Action

1. What is the benefit of pre-forgiveness if the person who has sinned against you never asks you for forgiveness?
2. Do you regularly ask those close to you for their observations about you? What are the advantages of speaking with those you sin against to understand the depth of the offense or any blind spots you may have?
3. Do you actively respond to the Spirit of God's illuminations as He guides you through the Word of God? What is something you have learned about yourself lately that you plan to address?
4. Are you practically speaking into the lives of your friends, helping them to repent well? Why is it necessary to build a relational bridge for them to have these in-depth conversations?

10

Past Sins

When my friend learned about our lack of forgiveness, he asked, "When you and Lucia realized you hadn't asked for forgiveness for several years, how did you work out the gospel in that situation? You couldn't go back and cover all your past sins against each other at that time, correct? So how do you handle forgiving sin over such an extended period?" My friend's question is vital because we all have a history with people. Sometimes, that history includes regrettable, sinful interactions, and if you don't have a sin plan that effectively neutralizes sin at the moment, the accumulative impact of unconfessed sin can weigh heavy on any relationship. Suppose you come to your senses and want to resolve past conflict with someone. How do you go about it?

Step One: Humble Heart

The first place to begin is in your heart as it relates to God. You do this by discerning what the Lord wants from you. All life problems begin vertically rather than horizontally. Therefore, you work to learn how to apply the greatest commandment practically—to love God most of all—before thinking about loving others second most of all (Matthew 22:36–40). That is where Lucia and I began, and King David gave us insight into how to prepare our hearts properly. He gives us a vital template to think about when working through relational brokenness.

> For you will not delight in sacrifice, or I would give it; you will not be pleased with a burnt offering. The sacrifices of God are a broken spirit; a broken and contrite heart, O God, you will not despise.
> (Psalm 51:16–17)

After many months of rebellion, the Lord started a persevering process of bringing David to Himself. When David thought about what was of first importance regarding his past sins, he did not begin with the horizontal works of reconciliation. Though a backward glance at David's nefarious activities saw a lot of sin that had strained and broken his most intimate relationships, the pressing thing on David's to-do list was a right heart before the Lord. He sat in the rubble of his blunders and begged God for clarity on where to begin fixing past mistakes (Psalm 51:2, 7). God wanted a contrite heart because David's brokenness with the Lord would form the foundation upon which he could rebuild redemptive horizontal relationships.

A genuinely repentant person is a broken and contrite person who has come to the end of himself (Luke 15:17), which starts with God's favor (James 4:6). David's thoughts were less on what he could do to fix his past mistakes and more on how he had sinned against God (Psalm 51:4). He was singing through quivering lips, "Nothing in my hand I bring; simply to Thy cross I cling." He intuitively knew that the only thing that would please God (Hebrews 11:6) would be if he rested in someone else's works. David's actions ruined his family, and more self-reliant efforts would only worsen matters, even if good intentions were behind them (Isaiah 64:6). He needed a better strategy, so he begged for God's help.

Step Two: Communication Levels

As you move into your horizontal relationships, remember there will always be a gap between who you are and what people know about you. You will need discernment in appropriately communicating your true self to others, including your past. Christians regularly survey the scene of their hearts while trying to cooperate with God in closing the distance between themselves and Jesus. However, it is unwise to reveal the totality of your entangled heart to every person you have offended (Jeremiah 17:9; Matthew 15:18-20). If your heart is contrite over your past, you should be willing to do whatever is necessary to make things right, including speaking to the right people in an appropriate way about your former sins. For example, I would not walk up to a man on the street and tell him some things that I tell my wife, and I do not tell my wife every sinful detail that floats through my brain. There are levels of transparency you want to factor into all your relationships. Your levels of transparency should resemble something like the following:

1. God knows everything about you (Hebrews 4:13).
2. Your spouse should know more about you than others (Ephesians 5:29).
3. Your spiritual overseers should know less than your spouse but more than others (Hebrews 13:17; Ephesians 4:12-15).
4. Some people in your local church should be your transparent friends.
5. Other acquaintances, neighbors, workmates, schoolmates, and friends should know less than the above relationships about you.

Step Three: Honest Talks

With a humble heart before the Lord and awareness of what to say to whom, these five tips will set things in motion as you work to reconcile your past with others.

- **Tip #1:** Make sure that people are pressing into your life and that you are aggressively building relationships with them to grow in a culture of honesty. Your primary, most intimate, and vulnerable relationship should be with your spouse.
- **Tip #2:** Everyone should know when they lie about something and hide things from their spouses. Maybe there are things you should not share, but you should be willing to examine your heart while holding your self-analysis loosely.
- **Tip #3:** Become biblically comfortable with the gap between who you are and your Christlike goals. Self-disclosure is a wisdom issue, but if you desire to reconcile your past with your spouse, the Lord will give you the illuminating favor you need on how to proceed and what to say (John 16:13; James 4:6). You will find a template for Christlikeness in Galatians 5:22–23.
- **Tip #4:** Daily seek to close the distance between you and your spouse, which may mean discussing past mistakes that interfere with your one flesh union. Think through any pockets of silence between you and ask the Spirit to help you speak about things that create silence between you.
- **Tip #5:** Read, digest, and practice the content on our website about communication. I have written scores of articles on koinonia. Become fluent in these matters, which you will do by practicing what you learn daily.

Step Four: Past Sins

> And Zacchaeus stood and said to the Lord, "Behold, Lord, the half of my goods I give to the poor. And if I have defrauded anyone of anything, I restore it fourfold."
>
> (Luke 19:8)

It is normal when a person encounters Jesus to begin thinking about past damages done (Ephesians 2:2). That kind of desire reflects the restorative heart that God gives us. As you ponder your past and how you'd like to reconcile current relationships, these eight things will help.

1. *Carefulness about applying unique, historical biblical events.* Though any passage of Scripture can have multiple applications, there is always only one point to a text. The Bible does not teach absolute rectification of all past sins. It is a common mistake for Christians to take a story from the Bible, map it over their lives, and do similar to what the historical figure in the Bible did. In the case of Zacchaeus, he was motivated to rectify his past sins. The point of the passage about Zacchaeus was his humility after meeting Jesus, not his unique-to-him works that flowed out of that humility. Though not everyone who met the Savior returned and rectified their past sins, some did.
2. *You may (or you may not) rectify past sins.* Several years ago, I tried to find my high school English teacher. I was a royal pain in her stressed-out rear end during my sophomore year. I went back to encourage her; I wanted her to know that her patience with me was not in vain. I also wanted to testify about the Lord's goodness in this former rebel teen's heart. I wanted her to know God

could make royal children out of royal pains. My reason for seeking her out was not instigated by what Zacchaeus did. It was not because of any unresolved multi-decade guilt or anxiety at work in my conscience. I did it because I respected her, wanted to glorify God, and hoped to encourage her. Regrettably, I could not find her. It's impossible to sift through your past sinfulness to make everything right. It's also illogical, impractical, and unwise. Perhaps there are situations where you can, and it is right to try to make it right with those you have sinned against.

3. *It may be possible to resolve current relationships.* If you have friends that you have sinned against, and it is possible to reach out to them, you should reach out to them and ask for their forgiveness. Spouses, parents, and children are a few of these relationships.

4. *It may be possible to reconcile with those suffering because of you.* If you have sinned against someone and the person is still struggling, it would be humble and correct to attempt to seek forgiveness from that person.

5. *If love cannot cover your sin.* Sometimes, love can cover our sins, and other transgressions can bleed through like a stain under white paint (1 Peter 4:8). If love does not cover your sins to where you can't be free from the guilt accompanying your actions, you should try to pursue restorative forgiveness.

6. *If your conscience is condemning you for your past sins.* Seeking advice for conscience-related matters is imperative. Many things other than the Bible can sway your conscience, so you must carefully discern a weak, hard, dull, or sensitive conscience. Genuine conviction comes from the Spirit of God, as the Word of God informs it. I have seen where

lousy religion created a false sense of guilt that was hard to discern from the Bible's genuine sense of guilt.
7. *If you hear from the Comforter, Canon, conscience, and community.* The four-legged biblical decision-making stool is your fail-safe to know if you are truly hearing from God. If the Spirit, God's Word, your conscience, and wise friends are on the same page, maybe you should seek to repair past wrongs.
8. *You cannot reconcile all relationships.* I have sinned against people and have sought reconciliation to resolve my misdeeds. Still, the other party was unwilling to cooperate. It happens. A typical situation where you cannot rectify past wrongs is after someone dies. Paul's language in Romans 12:18 is helpful when thinking about broken relationships. It should be the breadth of your responsibility to fix relational brokenness as much as it depends on you.

The Main Thing

After Lucia and I came to a contrite place in our hearts and marriage, most of the wrong stuff vaporized. Many of those things were no longer critical and not worth discussing. Then other things were shadows in the room or maybe pink elephants prancing about for our review. You asked, "When you and Lucia realized you hadn't asked for forgiveness for several years, how did you work out the gospel in that situation?" Two unalterable keys will let you know if the power of the gospel is working in your relationships:

- It should not be a problem to overlook offenses.
- Talking about the offenses you cannot ignore is also not a problem.

The gospel rightly understood and practically applied, does not minimize sin and does not allow you to linger on sin. The gospel obliterates past sins when the humble heart dials into its functional efficacy. As you think about your life, relationships, and the wrongs that may have come between you and others, please reflect on these questions. Perhaps sharing with a friend will help you clarify your responses to them.

Call to Action

1. Talk about how you would answer this: Is your primary objective to be right with God? What are your motives for making things right with God?
2. Is your heart humbly exposed and vulnerable before the Lord? Is your heart contrite, meaning this is not a damage control move? Do you have a genuinely broken heart over a past wrong?
3. Is your primary motive for cleaning up past messes because you love God more than anything else? Are you trying to pay for your sins, or are you resting in Christ's payment on your behalf?
4. How much distance is there between you and Christlikeness? Which way are you heading—away from Him or incrementally closing your gap?
5. How much should you reveal about your past? Think through something you should share and shouldn't share. Perhaps sharing those things with a friend would prove wise.
6. Who should you approach to reconcile past wrongs?
7. Is it possible to reconcile?
8. Can you overlook the offense?
9. Is your Spirit-illuminated, Bible-informed, conscience-affirming, and community advice telling you to go and reconcile?
10. Are you doing all you can to live in peace with that person?

11

Forgiving Yourself

Forgiving yourself is an odd teaching that has crept into Christians' understanding of sanctification. It's part of the culture's futile way of thinking, hoping to eliminate their sins. They must try because they sense the same shame we do, but because they reject God and His Word, they create policies and pathways to alleviate their soul noise, always leading down dead-end streets and box canyons. Without God, they blindly grope for the walls, making self-forgiveness a culturally common sense way of feeling psychologically better about themselves. "You just need to forgive yourself" is the usual way for people to apply this secular doctrine within their communities.

Who Is Sufficient?

Typically, a person who believes he needs to forgive himself has sinned in some way—hence the need for forgiveness. All sin requires transactional forgiveness to be free from it (Romans 10:13; 1 John 1:7–10). The need for forgiveness is a straightforward Christian doctrine: "I sin; I need forgiveness." The problem arises when the person seeking forgiveness is not seeking forgiveness from God or God alone. He is looking for something more besides God's forgiveness; he wants to be self-forgiving. Though he may know God will forgive him of his sins, he also believes self-forgiveness is required. "Yes, God has forgiven me, but I can't forgive myself for what I did" is a common response. Though this should be a self-evident heresy that distorts the gospel by adding to the forgiveness we receive from God alone, through Christ alone, based on the Bible alone, it is not clear to many Christians. The basic logic works like this:

- Christ Forgiving + Self-Forgiving = Heresy.
- Christ Forgiving + My Acceptance = Gospel

These self-forgiving people are unknowingly adding to the gospel (Galatians 1:8–9). It is like placing the lamb's blood above the doorpost and their blood too—a dangerous teaching (Exodus 12:7). The reason the perfect Lamb of God came to earth was to save us from our sins because we could not (John 1:29). An unclean thing cannot transform an unclean thing clean into a clean thing, making Christ's redemption a central plank in the gospel platform. Sin separates people from Christ, and if we are going to experience cleansing, God in the flesh must wash us whiter than snow by His blood (Ephesians 2:1–9). Jesus came and became a man, lived perfectly, died on the cross, and rose from the grave to conquer our sin and provide a means to free sinner-man from all guilt.

> In him we have redemption through his blood, the forgiveness of our trespasses, according to the riches of his grace.
> (Ephesians 1:7)

If sinner-man could forgive himself, he would not need a perfect sacrifice. If an imperfect sacrifice would do, who needs Christ? How convenient: "I can sin, forgive myself of my sin, and be free from my sin. I can live in a hermetically sealed, self-made, self-forgiving, redemptive world." The Bible teaches that only Christ can forgive us of our sins because we cannot forgive ourselves for our sins against an infinite, holy, almighty, and sovereign Lord. There is no biblical basis or need for this, but there is a self-created tension with some folks, as they struggle with self-forgiveness because they committed a sin. They have transgressed God's moral law and feel bad about their actions.

Lingering Conviction

This feeling is called conviction. It comes from the Spirit of God and the conscience, both good things to sense. Whenever we sin, there should be an appropriate and accompanying conviction. To feel bad about wrongs committed is a kindness from the Lord. Imagine being able to sin but not know, discern, or sense it. It would be like slicing your hand open and not feeling the pain. Pain in such an instance is mercy from God. Spiritual conviction is similar to physical discomfort. It allows us to respond to God, receive His forgiveness, and move on in the freedom that the power of the gospel offers (Galatians 5:1).

> *If we say we have no sin, we deceive ourselves, and the truth is not in us. If we confess our sins, he is faithful and just to forgive us our sins and to cleanse us from all unrighteousness.*
> (1 John 1:8–9)

Some Christians sometimes have difficulty receiving and resting in God's forensic and restorative forgiveness. They may even ask God to forgive them multiple times, but the lingering, residual feeling of conviction remains. This feeling is a false sensation of a person not resting in the gospel's transformative power. Their lack of gospel trust disables them from fully appropriating the undeserved favor God provides. These unbelieving Christians (Mark 9:24) continue to struggle with ongoing issues like guilt, remorse, shame, and embarrassment. Their self-imposed guilt may even drive them to isolate themselves from others by hiding the complete truth about what is happening internally. Like their predecessor Adam, they cover themselves with fig leaves.

> Then the eyes of both were opened, and they knew that they were naked. And they sewed fig leaves together and made themselves loincloths.
> (Genesis 3:7)

Hiding unresolved guilt issues complicates the original sin as they pursue transgressive escapes to find relief from the guilt. Rather than running to God, they entangle themselves in a godless orbit of temptations that pushes them into a spiral of self-perpetuating dysfunction. The gospel's full power becomes marginalized in their lives because their view of themselves, God, and His gospel is limited and smallish. This worldview is the appeal of the self-esteem movement, a person who spends an inordinate amount of time thinking about themselves rather than God (Philippians 2:3–5).

Self-Esteem Gospel

- Self-esteem teaches us to think highly of ourselves. Christianity teaches us to think highly of others.
- Self-esteem teaches us to be all we can be. Christianity teaches us to make others great.
- Self-esteem teaches us to be independent. Christianity teaches us to be interdependent.
- Self-esteem teaches us to be competitive. Christianity teaches us to elevate others.
- Self-esteem teaches us not to be self-critical. Christianity teaches us to own our depravity.

The self-esteem movement is counter-productive to the Christian way of thinking. It leads to more and more introspection and individualism, which has an incarcerating effect on the mind. Can anyone think more about themselves and feel better about themselves because of their introspective reflections? The gospel frees us from ourselves while motivating us to focus more on God and others. The self-forgiver is intuitively self-focused. All he can think about is what he did, how bad he feels about what he did, and how God would never forgive such an awful person. Self-esteem makes man and his problems big and God and His efficacious power small.

Looking at Me

The Bible category for self-esteem is self-righteousness. Let me illustrate: imagine a person being two people. Let's say the person is me. In this illustration, I am person A, and I am person B. I am representing both people. Now, let's say person A commits adultery, and person B, also me, is in disbelief over what person A did. In other words, I am shocked at what I did. "Dear God, I can't believe I did that." In addition to being shocked, I am embarrassed, angry, frustrated, confused, and ashamed of what I did. My self-esteem gospel tells me to think highly of myself (person B), but my reality tells me I have a problem (person A). I'm in a tailspin. Why?

- Self-esteem says, "I am somebody. I am great. I can do all things through me who strengthens me."
- The Bible says, "I am a sinner, totally depraved, and capable of many other things that are worse than adultery."

Only a person with a high view of himself would be shocked at what he did: "It is so bad that I can't get over it." No Christian should be surprised when he sins. Though we are saints, we also choose to sin on occasion. We are fallen people living in a fallen world, and at times we are tempted to yield to the temptation to sin—a sad fact of life. If we regularly imbibe the counter-productive self-esteem model, we will constantly be shrinking into someone who finds it hard to accept their sinfulness. While we continually caress and massage ourselves upward by maintaining our high thoughts about ourselves, our sin will also confront us, colliding in our minds like a roller coaster of evil and conflicted thoughts (James 1:5–8).

The self-esteem model teaches a person to ignore weaknesses and wrongs. Thus, when the certainty of our Adamic tendencies comes to roost, we will be surprised, shocked, disbelieving, and discouraged. The Christian's counter to this worldview is to regularly soak in the Scripture's view that we are saints who sin. This view will prepare us to face the reality of who we are before God and others. Though we will experience guilt and conviction after we sin, our actions will not throw us into a ditch. We can fast-track to the only one who can fully and freely forgive us. The Bible does not have a high view of humans. The Bible has a dismal and dark view of who we are and the dastardly things we can do. Whenever the Bible talks about our propensities outside of the grace of God, its view of man is low—even pronouncing eternal torment on those who reject God ultimately. (See Romans 3:10–12 and Revelation 20:15.)

Price of Forgiveness

Self-esteem—biblically defined as self-righteousness—can only lead to one conclusion: we must go outside the Bible's boundaries for a solution. Thus, the self-esteemer can never be free. He will live with the nagging, ongoing residual effect of guilt and shame because of his unwillingness to embrace a sober assessment of who he is—a born-again sinner. The battles of guilt and shame that reject the gospel's cure will always motivate other measures like self-forgiveness.

> I asked Christ to forgive me, and I believe He did, but I still struggle with what I did, so I just need to forgive myself.

If you have difficulty embracing your sins or accepting the poor view of yourself that your sins affirm, you will have difficulty obtaining a gospel cleanse. Christ came for sinners, not people who can't believe they did such a thing or won't own the truth about their sinful actions (Luke 5:32). All sin is against God, and only God can forgive sin. Let me illustrate by giving you a truth and an analogy.

- **TRUTH:** The person we sin against—the Lord—is the one who determines the price to pay to cover the offense.
- **ANALOGY:** If you cause a car accident, you do not determine what you will pay to make amends for your mistake. The insurance company assesses the damages and lets you know what you must pay.

This analogy is proximate to how forgiveness works with God. He always determines what it will take to cover the offense—not you, the offender. The Lord made that decision a long time ago when He sent His one and only Son to die on the cross for our sins (John 1:29, 3:7, 3:16). You or I do not tell the "Insurance Agent" what we must pay, including an additional sacrifice for the sins we commit. Imagine a friend paying for your meal at a restaurant. Though you appreciate it, you decide to also pay for the meal—in addition to his payment. You do not need to pay for something someone has already paid; you do not need to forgive yourself after God has forgiven you. The real question is, "Can you rest in His forgiveness?"

Call to Action

The gospel came to take care of your sin problems because you could not. Your job should be straightforward: apply the gospel to your life. You must ask, receive, and apply God's forgiveness. Then rest in His gospel goodness. If you are like me, a person who can become overly shocked by personal sin, maybe you need to repent of self-righteousness. Sometimes I forget how Jesus is enough for all my sin. How about you?

1. Are you able to rest in God's forgiveness? What does that mean, practically speaking? How is the gospel lowering your soul noise? What does the peace of God mean to you?
2. Why do you sense the need to forgive yourself when an infinite God gave you an infinite gift to pay for your infinite offense against Him? What can you add to infinity? Talk about why it's wrong to remove your guilt by something more than Christ's sacrifice.
3. What is going on in your thinking that hinders you from trusting and resting in the Lord? What compels you to add to the gospel? Why isn't God's forgiveness enough?
4. Does a person mean something else when he says that he needs to forgive himself? What is he attempting to describe? If you sense guilt in your soul that continues, what is the solution, which we know is not self-forgiveness?
5. If you believe you must forgive yourself, will you support that belief with God's Word? What verse or direct teaching of Scripture support your view? Will you share your findings with a biblically literate person, who will not rubber-stamp your view, but engage you with God's Word?

Conclusion

A happy home does not just happen. Like all good things, you must have a plan and be willing to execute the hard work necessary for a biblically-sound home (Luke 14:27). The good news is that Christians have the schematic for happiness, which starts with confession and moves into forgiveness. The crucial concern centers on whether we'll do the hard work of confessing our transgressions and forgiving each other. The couple that understands this path to reconciliation and practices it regularly will not stop until they become the beneficiaries of a happy home.

Confession and Happiness

Confession, forgiveness, and reconciliation are elements that lead you down the path to happiness (Deuteronomy 33:29). If you want a happy home, you must know how to clean up your messes and practice it daily. During the first five years of our marriage, I never asked my wife to forgive me for any sins I committed against her. Think about it. What I just said is staggering. Let me state the obvious: my view of God, humanity, and the doctrine of sin was dysfunctional. My gospel understanding and practices suffered from a failure to thrive (Hebrews 5:12–14; 1 Peter 2:2–3).

Yikes!

I'm not going to rationalize or provide a weak attempt

to minimize the contradiction of my life back then. But I have observed through counseling many Christians that after I ask them about their forgiveness practices in the home, nearly all of them have said they do not regularly do it. They do not pursue each other in humility, which their lack of reciprocal ownership of sin, mutual confession, and selfless forgiveness affirms. The oddity of this unchristian behavior is stunning when viewed through the lens of our imitate-able gospel (1 Corinthians 11:1). The Lord's gospel loudly proclaims a not guilty verdict to all regenerated people (John 3:7).

Sadly, I could not perceive and apply the benefits of His grace (Psalm 103:1-2) during the early part of our marriage (James 4:6). Perhaps you can do a quick temperature check of your home and closest relationships to assess how you are doing.

- How often do you ask your family members to forgive you for things you've done wrong?
- Would you characterize your home as a place where confession and forgiveness regularly happen?
- Are all the members of your home committed to practicing confession and forgiveness?
- Are you more aware of what you do wrong or what other family members do wrong (Matthew 7:3-5)?

Your answers to my questions will direct you to what you should do next.

Forgiveness and Happiness

The most radical, life-changing, relationship-building question you will ever ask another person is, "Will you forgive me?" That is how our revolutionary, life-changing, relationship-building experience with God began. The process is no different for His image bearers (Genesis 1:27;

Ephesians 5:1). A Christian who does not regularly ask for forgiveness is like the son of a millionaire unaware of his daddy's fortune. Or even worse, he knows of his daddy's fortune but refuses to benefit from those riches (1 Peter 1:4). Forgiveness is a free and unlimited mercy from the Lord.

Still, it requires humility to access it, whether asking or granting. "Will you forgive me?" is not a complex question, but it is not one of the common questions asked within the Christian community—especially in our homes and local churches. The person not regularly asking for forgiveness is either self-deceived, a pretender, or in denial of the doctrine of sin. A forgiven person—authentically living in the grace of that forgiveness—is ready, willing, and able to ask for forgiveness and grant it—attitudinally or transactionally.

As you think about your life and home in the context of this book, I hope these final thoughts will give you the encouragement you need to begin building a confessional home that takes sin seriously, the gospel practically, your relationships deeper, and God's fame as your primary motivation. If you are serious about change and want to partner with a friend in that process, I appeal to you to work through all the questions throughout this book. As you do that, consider these seven steps.

Seven Simple Steps

1. **BE HONEST:** You know when you sin (1 John 1:7–10; Romans 2:14–15; Hebrews 4:7–8). Don't fall for the traps of justification, rationalization, alleviation, or blaming. Name it; claim it; confess your sins to God and all others in the sphere of offense.
2. **SPIRIT-WALKING:** Step into the reality of what you did when you sense God's illumination; don't run from it. Pray for heightened sensitivity to the Spirit of God and obey Him in all things. Practice a life of honesty

and integrity. When He speaks, listen and act.
3. **PRACTICE FORGIVENESS:** Don't say I'm sorry or apologize when talking about a transgression. Push the biblical envelope by pursuing radical reconciliation. Ask for forgiveness, and don't settle for anything less.
4. **GOD FIRST:** Don't ask others to forgive you while not asking God first. All sin is a sin against the Lord. Sometimes we sin against others too. If you sin against others, you must ask both for forgiveness.
5. **BE SPECIFIC:** "Will you forgive me for [this specific thing]?" Let them know that you know how you have sinned. Convince them that you have sinned. Do not let them let you off the hook. Convince them to forgive you as you bring a compelling argument against yourself. Be persuasive and unrelenting in your pursuit of forgiveness.
6. **TAP OUT:** Give up your rights by submitting yourself to the authority of God and His Word. Choose brokenness until you find release from your sins and restoration to those you offended. (Read Psalm 51.) Do not settle for anything less.
7. **DON'T FORGET:** There is power in forgiveness. After the Father executed His Son on the cross (Isaiah 53:10) for your sin and mine, He made it possible for any person to experience release from the guilt and punishment that all sin deserves (Romans 6:23).

As a Christian, you and I have the grace-empowered privilege to live daily in a guilt-free environment if we choose to be honest with ourselves, God, and others. After Lucia and I began to see the gospel with more practical clarity, we started to live in the restored sanctification sweet spot that radically changed our home. We replaced the guilt, burden, shame, unresolved conflict, and proverbial pink elephants flying around the room with love, joy, peace, hope, and the mercy Christ offers through His gospel. Do not be like the rich kid who is clueless about or resistant to what his daddy possesses. Step up to your inheritance by asking your family to forgive you whenever you sin against them. Be radical. Step into the enjoyment of your Christian experience with others.

Call to Action

1. Describe your family's sin plan. Some elements should be conviction, confession, pre-forgiveness, forgiveness, post-forgiveness, reconciliation, and restoration. What are a few other features that you incorporate into your sin plan? I'm speaking of the doctrine of repentance, the plan that changes our lives and relationships.
2. Do you have a confessional home? What does that mean? Think through the rhythm of confession in your home. There should be a steady and comfortable beat of confession, something you're so used to doing that is not odd but welcomed.
3. Why is asking for forgiveness better than saying, "I'm sorry?"
4. Do you have a happy home? Is there relational warmth wafting from room to room? If not, what is one thing you will do to cooperate with the Lord to build a happy home?
5. Who are you going to ask to walk with you on this journey?

About the Author

Rick Thomas launched the Life Over Coffee global training network in 2008 to bring hope and help for you and others by creating resources that spark conversations for transformation. His primary responsibilities are resource creation and leadership development, which he does through speaking, writing, podcasting, and educating. In 1990 he earned a BA in Theology and, in 1991, a BS in Education. In 1993, he received his ordination into Christian ministry, and in 2000, he graduated with an MA in Counseling from The Master's University. In 2006, he was recognized as a Fellow of the Association of Certified Biblical Counselors (ACBC).

Other Books Available from Life Over Coffee

Boasting in Weakness
Centering Your Marriage on Christ
Communication
Complete Marriage
Don't Apologize
Exchange the Truth for a Lie
Help My Marriage Has Grown Cold
Identity Crisis
Local Church
Loving Me
Mad
Marriage Devotion We Are One
Politics and Culture
Parenting Devotion from Zero to Adulthood
Sex, Temptation, and Modesty
Storm Hurler
The Cyber Effect
The Talk
Wives Leading
You Decide

www.ingramcontent.com/pod-product-compliance
Lightning Source LLC
Chambersburg PA
CBHW052148070526
44585CB00017B/2027